INTRODUCING THE OLD TESTAMENT

Zondervan Books by Tremper Longman III

"Amos" and "Obadiah" (co-author) in
Expositor's Bible Commentary, Revised Edition

"Daniel" in *The NIV Application Commentary*

An Introduction to the Old Testament

"Proverbs" in *Zondervan Illustrated Bible
Backgrounds Commentary, Old Testament*

*Show Them No Mercy: Four Views on God
and Canaanite Genocide* (editor)

a short guide to its history and message

INTRODUCING THE OLD TESTAMENT

tremper
LONGMAN III

ZONDERVAN®

ZONDERVAN.com/
AUTHORTRACKER
follow your favorite authors

We want to hear from you. Please send your comments about this book to us in care of zreview@zondervan.com. Thank you.

ZONDERVAN

Introducing the Old Testament
An abridgment of *An Introduction to the Old Testament*
Copyright © 1994, 2006, 2012 by Tremper Longman III

This title is also available as a Zondervan ebook.
Visit www.zondervan.com/ebooks.

Requests for information should be addressed to:

Zondervan, *Grand Rapids, Michigan* 49530

Library of Congress Cataloging-in-Publication Data

Longman, Tremper.
    Introducing the Old Testament : a short guide to its history and message /
Tremper Longman III.
        pages cm
    ISBN 978-0-310-29148-0 (softcover)
    1. Bible. O.T.—Introductions. I. Title.
BS1140.3.L662 2012
221.6'1—dc23   2012000765

Cover photography: Masterfile
Interior design: Matthew Van Zomeren

Printed in the United States of America

HB 01.16.2020

CONTENTS

ABBREVIATIONS

AB	Anchor Bible
Apollos	Apollos Old Testament Commentary Series
BCOTWP	Baker Commentary on the Old Testament Wisdom and Psalms
BJS	Brown Judaic Studies
CsBC	Cornerstone Biblical Commentary Series
DSB	Daily Study Bible
EBC-R	Expositor's Bible Commentary: Revised Edition
Interp	Interpretation: A Bible Commentary for Teaching and Preaching
NAC	New American Commentary
NCB	New Century Bible
NIBCOT	New International Bible Commentary, Old Testament
NICOT	New International Commentary on the Old Testament
NIVAC	NIV Application Commentary
OTL	Old Testament Library Commentary Series
SHBC	Smith and Helwys Bible Commentary
TOTC	Tyndale Old Testament Commentaries
UBCS	Understanding the Bible Commentary Series
WBC	Word Bible Commentary
ZIBBC	Zondervan Illustrated Bible Backgrounds Commentary

chapter one

THINKING ABOUT THE STUDY OF THE OLD TESTAMENT

The Old Testament contains those books written before the time of Jesus that are considered by the church to be the Word of God and thus, along with the New Testament, an authoritative guide to faith and practice. Unfortunately, many Christians ignore the Old Testament, even though it constitutes more than three-quarters of the Bible, because it is long, strange, and difficult. However, a knowledge of the Old Testament deepens our understanding of Jesus and the gospel and, though it is not always easy, studying it can enrich our spiritual life and knowledge of God.

About This Book

This book intends to provide the literary, historical, and theological background to the reading of the individual books of the Old Testament. Each chapter treats a single book of the Old Testament, and most chapters have the following structure (though not necessarily in the same order):

1. Content: What is the book about?
2. Authorship and Date: Who wrote the book and when?
3. Genre: What is the style of literature of the book?
4. Connections: How does the book anticipate the gospel?

There is also a short excursus exploring the genre of theological history (presented after the chapter on Esther). Much of the Old Testament is theological history; thus we give it a general treatment in the excursus while describing specific issues in the book chapters. Other genres (law, poetry, wisdom, prophecy, apocalyptic) are described in the relevant chapters.

Each chapter ends with references to further resources and then questions. What follows are some general resources for the study of the Old Testament.

Introductory

The NLT Study Bible. Wheaton, IL: Tyndale House, 2008.
The NIV Study Bible. Grand Rapids: Zondervan, 2011.

Intermediate

Alexander, T. Desmond, and D. W. Baker, eds. *Dictionary of the Pentateuch.* Downers Grove, IL: InterVarsity Press, 2003.

Arnold, B., and H. G. M. Williamson, eds. *Dictionary of the Historical Books.* Downers Grove, IL: InterVarsity Press, 2005.

Boda, M., and G. McConville, eds. *Dictionary of the Prophets.* Downers Grove, IL: InterVarsity Press, 2012.

Longman III, T., and P. Enns, eds. *Dictionary of Wisdom, Poetry and Writings.* Downers Grove, IL: InterVarsity Press, 2008.

Advanced

Longman III, T., and R. B. Dillard. *Introduction to the Old Testament.* 2nd ed. Grand Rapids: Zondervan, 2006.

chapter two

THE BOOK
OF GENESIS

Content: What Is Genesis About?

The title Genesis means "Beginnings," and this book is indeed
about beginnings: the beginnings of the cosmos, human beings, sin,
a people chosen by God, and much more. Genesis is the first part of
what is really a five-part literary composition known as the Torah or
Pentateuch. The main story of the Pentateuch concerns the founding
of Israel as a nation emerging from Egypt and traveling toward the
Promised Land. Genesis is the prequel or introduction to this great
story.

We can divide the contents of the book of Genesis into three
parts, beginning with an account of primordial history (Gen. 1–11)
that describes the creation of the world and humanity (Gen. 1–2).
The account of creation is written using highly figurative language
that bears similarity and contrasts with other ancient Near Eastern
creation accounts from Mesopotamia (Enuma Elish; Atrahasis),
Canaan (Baal and Anat), and Egypt (the Memphite Theology in
particular). The purpose is not to explain *how* God created creation,
but to proclaim that it was Yahweh rather than one of the other creation gods of the ancient Near East. The creation text also informs
its readers about the nature of God (who is both transcendent and
immanent), the dignified status of both men and women in the
world, and the importance of marriage, work, and Sabbath. The
creation accounts reveal that God created a good physical universe,
and the account of Adam and Eve's rebellion explains how sin and
death came into the world (Gen. 3). The evil that people experience
in themselves and from each other has nothing to do with how God

created human beings, but rather with human choice to rebel rather than to submit to God.

The remainder of the primordial history contains both genealogies and three more stories. These stories all follow a similar pattern that reflects a pattern established in Genesis 3.

(1) Sin

Adam and Eve disobey God by eating from the tree of the knowledge of good and evil (3:6–7)
Cain murders his brother Abel (4:8)
Humanity is completely evil (6:5, 11–12)
People settle down and build a city and a tower that is intended to reach the heavens (11:2–5)

(2) God announces judgment

The serpent, Eve, and Adam are rebuked (3:14–19)
Cain must wander (4:11–12)
The flood is proclaimed (6:7, 13–21)
Language is confused (11:6–7)

(3) A token of grace, a sign of God's continued involvement

Clothes (3:21)
A mark to protect Cain from violence (4:15)
Noah and the ark (6:8, 18–22)
Languages rather than complete confusion (chap. 10)

(4) The execution of judgment

Expelled from Eden and made subject to death (3:22–24)
Driven farther from Eden and made a wanderer (4:16)
Destroyed by the floodwaters (7:6–24)
Scattered and confused by language (11:8–9)

Up to this point in the book, Genesis focuses on the whole of creation and all of humanity. These stories depict humans as thoroughly sinful and deserving of punishment. God is described as one who judges sin, but also as gracious as he continues to pursue reconciliation with his human creatures.

The second of the three major sections of Genesis focuses on the patriarchs Abraham, Isaac, and Jacob (chaps. 12–36). Genesis 12:1–3 is one of the most important passages in the Bible. It describes God's command that Abraham leave his homeland and travel to Canaan, and in return, God promises to make a great nation from Abraham, implying that he will have land as well as numerous descendants. In addition, God will bless Abraham and his descendants and also, through them, "all peoples on earth."

Abraham is thus the father of the chosen people. For the most part, his life story follows his faith struggle as he encounters threats and obstacles to the fulfillment of the promises, especially the promise that he will have many descendants. To have many descendants, he has to have a child, but many years pass and still Abraham has no heir. God comes back to reaffirm his covenant promise to the patriarch (chaps. 15, 17), but time and time again Abraham keeps trying to manufacture his own heir. Once he suggests that he adopt his household servant Eliezer (15:2–3), and on another occasion he takes a secondary wife, Hagar, who gives birth to Ishmael (16; 17:18). God, though, continues to assure him that he will have his own child through whom the covenant promises will continue. Finally, in their advanced old age, Abraham and Sarah have Isaac (21:1–7). Born well beyond the natural age for childbearing, Isaac is clearly a gift from God. Even so, in a final and ultimate test of Abraham's faith, God commands him to take his son and sacrifice him on Mount Moriah (chap. 22). At this point in his life, Abraham's faith is strong and, though God stays his hand before he kills Isaac, Abraham shows his steely confidence in God (see Heb. 11:17–19).

The covenant promises are passed down to Isaac and then to his son Jacob. Isaac is a rather undeveloped character in Genesis, while Jacob, the trickster who himself is tricked on occasion, is rather colorful. Jacob struggles in his relationship with God, culminating in a wrestling match with him, after which God changes his name to "Israel," the future name of the people of God (32:22–32). Israel and his two wives and two concubines give birth to twelve sons, who give their names to the future twelve tribes of Israel.

The concluding part of Genesis (chaps. 37–50) concerns Joseph, one of the twelve sons of Jacob. This story serves as a bridge between Genesis and Exodus, since it explains how the descendants of Abraham make their way down to Egypt. The Joseph story is filled with family intrigue. Jacob has his favorite son, Joseph, and thus his siblings are extremely jealous, and at their first opportunity they sell him to traders who take him down to Egypt, where he serves as a slave. Although experiencing evil at the hands of his brothers, his Egyptian owners, and others, Joseph at the end of his life sees the guiding hand of divine providence that used these horrible experiences to save his family, the family of promise, from the deadly effects of a severe famine. Joseph articulates this understanding to his brothers after the death of his father, Jacob: "You intended to harm me, but God intended it for good to accomplish what is now being done, the saving of many lives" (50:20).

The book of Genesis ends with the death of Joseph, but it anticipates the continuation of the story in the book of Exodus when Joseph makes his brothers promise that they will take his embalmed body back to the Promised Land in the future (50:22–26).

Authorship and Date: Who Wrote Genesis and When?

The question of the authorship of Genesis is bound up with the question of the Pentateuch as a whole, so that will be the subject of this section, and later chapters will refer back here. The authorship of the Pentateuch, perhaps surprising to some readers, is one of the most hotly debated subjects of Old Testament scholarship. On the one side are those who want to defend the viewpoint that Moses wrote the Pentateuch. On the other side are those who argue that Moses wrote no part of the Pentateuch, but rather that the Pentateuch is the result of a long history of composition that may have begun as early as the time of the United Monarchy (tenth century BC) but did not end until the postexilic period. Of course, there are many variations on these schools of thought, particularly the second.

Analysis of the issue should begin with the observation that the Pentateuch is technically anonymous. No one is ever named as the author of the Pentateuch within the Pentateuch itself. However, the Pentateuch does describe Moses writing down law (Ex. 24:4; 34:27), narrative (Ex. 17:4; Num. 33:2), and a song (Deut. 31:22; see Deut. 32), so it does picture Moses in a writing capacity — though, again, these passages may not be construed as indicating that Moses wrote the entirety or even the majority of the Pentateuch. Even so, later Scripture looks back on a body of writing that is clearly associated with the Pentateuch and refers to it by such titles as the "Book of Moses" (2 Chron. 25:4; Ezra 6:18; Neh. 13:1; see also Josh. 1:7, 8). In the New Testament, Jesus and the composers of the Gospels associated much, if not all, of the Pentateuch with Moses (Matt. 19:7; 22:24; Mark 7:10; 12:26; John 1:17; 5:46; 7:23).

These are the strongest reasons to think that Moses was involved in the composition of the Pentateuch, but they do not constitute evidence that he wrote it in its entirety. Indeed, most defenders of Mosaic authorship recognize that there are certain texts that Moses could not have written, most clearly the account of his death in Deuteronomy 34. Since these texts were obviously written after Moses' life, there is no good principal reason to think that other texts that are not so easily recognized were also written later in the history of Israel, perhaps even as late as the postexilic period. On the one hand, Moses is presented as an authority figure in the book. Thus, if he was not involved at all in the writing of the Pentateuch — or at least if the traditions about his involvement in the history of Israel (particularly the receiving of the law) are not true — then there are some legitimate theological questions that can be raised. On the other hand, the ultimate authority of these materials rests not on Moses' authority, but on God's.

Many scholars strongly believe that Moses was not involved in the composition of the Pentateuch, but instead it is a result of a process that lasted many centuries. While, as mentioned, there are a number of alternate theories for the production of the Pentateuch, the classic Documentary Hypothesis is the default viewpoint still held and taught by many today.

The modern era of the study of sources in the Pentateuch began when Jewish philosopher Baruch Spinoza (1632 – 77) questioned its authorial unity, but it was Jean Astruc (1684 – 1766) who first proposed sources. He attempted to defend Mosaic authorship by suggesting that Moses himself used a source. The Mosaic material could be distinguished from the source by the use of the divine name Yahweh rather than Elohim. Very soon after Astruc, however, the search for the original sources of the Pentateuch led many scholars to completely disassociate it from Moses. The classic source-critical analysis of the Pentateuch now known as the Documentary Hypothesis was formulated by Julius Wellhausen in the 1880s. He used four basic criteria to distinguish the sources from each other: (1) the divine names Elohim and Yahweh, (2) double stories (for instance, the two accounts of creation in Gen. 1:1 – 2:4a and 2:4b – 25), (3) double namings (for instance, the nomads said to have taken Joseph to Egypt are called Ishmaelites [Gen. 37:25] and Midianites [Gen. 37:28]), and

(4) different theology (for instance, monotheism versus henotheism, or a central altar versus multiple altars).

Wellhausen concluded that there were four sources that came together over time to produce the Pentateuch. The oldest source was J, the Jahwist. Often dated to the tenth century BC and considered a southern source, J was a captivating storyteller, describing God in larger-than-life human terms. A good example of J's style and theology may be seen in Genesis 2 and 3, the second creation account and the story of Adam and Eve's rebellion. The J source may be found intermittently up through the book of Numbers. The second source was E, the Elohist. Often dated to the ninth century BC and considered a northern source, E is more fragmentary than J, distinguished by its use of Elohim rather than Yahweh to refer to God. The third source was D, the Deuteronomist. Dated to a specific time in the late seventh century BC because of its association with the discovery of a law book in the temple during Josiah's reforms (2 Kings 22–23), D is mostly associated with the book of Deuteronomy, so its distinctive theological perspective may be found in the chapter on Deuteronomy. The final source is P, the Priestly source, so named because much of its content would be of interest to the priestly class (genealogies, sacrifices, sacred festivals, purity laws, etc.). It is often dated to the exilic or postexilic period.

This traditional view of the Documentary Hypothesis is still widely held today. Interest in source criticism seems to have waned in the period 1980 to 1995 because scholars began to focus on the final form of the text regardless of its possible diachronic origins. This interest came about through the influence of both canonical readings of the text and an emphasis on the application of literary methods to the study of the Old Testament. This concern with the final form of the text continues today, but is coupled with a renewed commitment to analyzing the sources that combined to produce the final form.

While Wellhausen's conclusions continue to be widely held, there are many variations among scholars that are intensely debated. For example, some scholars hold that it is not possible to distinguish E from J. Others would take D and/or P as indicating a redactional perspective rather than an original separate source. Some speak in general terms of P and non-P, finding it hard to distinguish the other sources.

Furthermore, many remain skeptical of the whole endeavor of trying to find sources in this way, and they continue to defend an essential Mosaic authorship of the Pentateuch, proposing alternate reasons for the criteria that lead many to propose sources. Such a view must, however, recognize that there are sources of a different type in the Pentateuch (introduced by the formula *'elleh toledot* PN, "This is the account of PN," where PN is the personal name of a person whose descendants will be the subject of the following section [2:4; 5:1; 6:9; 10:1; 11:10, 27; 25:12, 19; 36:1, 9]). These indicate the use of oral and/or written sources (see 5:1) for the writing of the book of Genesis. In addition, as noted above, the presence of the so-called post-Mosaica makes clear that the composition of the Pentateuch did not come to a close with the death of Moses. The amount of material that postdates Moses in the Pentateuch is unclear.

Genre: What Style of Literature Is Genesis?

Whether Genesis was written in large part by Moses using sources or later, the book of Genesis gives an account of the past—indeed, reaching back to the far distant past, even the creation of the cosmos. Thus the book can rightly be called a work of history, if by history is meant a recounting of past events.

However, like all history writing, Genesis recounts the past in order to help explain the present and from a certain focus that is generated by later interests. Take, for instance, the creation narratives. They make a bold historical claim: Yahweh (and not any other god) created creation. The creation narratives clearly have a theological, and not a scientific, interest. Since the creation accounts (and the rest of the primeval history [chaps. 1–11]) use a high degree of figurative language and interact extensively with ancient Near Eastern literature, it is an error to read these chapters to discover *how* God created the universe.

Beginning with Abraham, the reader can detect a clear shift in narrative style. Time slows down and the scope of the narrative radically narrows. While Genesis 1–11 covers the whole world from creation up to Abraham (an undetermined, but enormous period of time), the focus narrows to one individual, Abraham, whose life is then followed for the next fourteen chapters. Thus the composer signals a more intense interest in historical detail that continues until the end of the book.

That is not to deny that literary and theological concerns shape the presentation of the patriarchs and Joseph. The Abraham narrative is concerned with the patriarchs' response to the covenant promises, and Joseph's life is told in a way that highlights the providence of God as he preserves the people of promise through a harrowing famine.

Connections: How Does Genesis Anticipate the Gospel?

The connections between the book of Genesis and the New Testament are manifold; accordingly, we can only highlight a few. Romans 5:12–21 describes Christ as a second Adam. The first Adam brought sin and death into the world by his disobedience, while the second Adam, Christ, brings life through his righteousness (see also 1 Cor. 15:45–49 for an Adam and Christ analogy).

Paul also draws a connection between Jesus and Abraham in Galatians 3:15–22, and it is a rather surprising one at that. Paul reminds his readers of the promises God made to Abraham, especially the promise of "seed." He emphasizes the fact that God's promised seed is singular and therefore does not point to many descendants, but rather to only one, whom he identifies as none other than Christ. Jesus is the "seed" anticipated by the promise to Abraham. This is surprising in that the book of Genesis itself makes it clear that the promise of "seed" does indeed point to the numerous descendants of Abraham (for instance, Gen. 15:5). Paul as an expert in the Old Testament would surely have known this. What Paul is doing is exploiting the collective singular to make an important theological point. Jesus is the ultimate fulfillment of the Abrahamic promise, and those who are in union with Christ are the true children of Abraham (Gal. 3:29).

The Joseph story also anticipates Christ in that Joseph's life illustrates God's providence whereby he can even use the evil acts of people to bring about salvation. In Joseph's case, God used his brothers, Potiphar's wife, and others to put him in a place where he could provide for his family during a famine. In the case of Christ, God used the actions of evil men who nailed Jesus to the cross in order to bring salvation to the world (Acts 2:22–24).

Recommended Resources

Duguid, I. M. *Living in the Gap between Promise and Reality: The Gospel according to Abraham.* Phillipsburg, NJ: P and R Publishing, 1999.

_____. *Living in the Grip of Relentless Grace: The Gospel according to Isaac and Jacob*. Phillipsburg, NJ: P and R Publishing, 2002.

Longman, T. *How to Read Genesis*. Downers Grove, IL: InterVarsity Press, 2005.

Waltke, B. K. *Genesis*. Grand Rapids: Zondervan, 2001.

Walton, J. H. "Genesis." Pages 2–159 in ZIBBC 1. Edited by J. H. Walton. Grand Rapids: Zondervan, 2009.

Questions for Review and Discussion

1. How does Genesis relate to the rest of the Pentateuch?
2. What does the creation story teach us about God, ourselves, and our world?
3. How does the story of Abraham inform us about the nature of faith?
4. What does the Joseph narrative tell us about the nature of divine providence?
5. Who wrote the Pentateuch?
6. Read Galatians 3:15–22 yourself and see if you agree with the perspective offered in this chapter.

chapter three

THE BOOK OF EXODUS

Content: What Is Exodus About?

The book of Exodus is the second chapter of the Pentateuch and concerns three weighty biblical-theological themes:

God delivers Israel from Egyptian bondage (Exodus, chaps. 1–18)

God gives Israel the law (Law, chaps. 19–24)

God provides the tabernacle for Israel (Presence of God, chaps. 25–50)

The action of the book opens after a period of some time since the death of Joseph, which closed the book of Genesis. The situation for God's people has changed dramatically since the time of Joseph. In the first place, Jacob's extended family has become "extremely numerous" (Exod. 1:5). But ominously, a "new king" of Egypt has come to perceive the Israelites as a threat. Accordingly, he orders their enslavement, putting them to work to build two store cities (1:11). He further orders the death of all newborn baby boys, although the midwives do not see this mandate carried out, and thus Moses, the future savior of Israel, is born (2:1–10). However, a time comes when Moses' mother can no longer keep his presence hidden, so she places him in a reed basket that floats down the Nile until Pharaoh's daughter discovers it and raises the baby Moses, with his mother serving as the wet nurse. The irony, of course, is that the future deliverer of Israel is raised in the household of the oppressive Pharaoh himself. Interestingly, the Sargon Birth Legend tells a similar story about Sargon the Great, who at birth was placed in a basket and floated down the Euphrates River, where his basket was picked up by a man who raised him as his own child. The similarity gives the impression that both mothers were acting according to a common cultural convention under similar circumstances. They believed that by placing their children on the water they were committing them to the care and protection of their respective deities.

After killing an Egyptian who was beating a Hebrew slave, Moses realizes that his relationship with Pharaoh's household will not protect him, so he flees to Midian, where he enters the household of Jethro by marrying his daughter Zipporah. While Moses is shepherding his father-in-law's flocks, God appears to him in a burning bush and commissions him and his brother Aaron to return to insist on the release of Israel from its enslavement. In the process, God speaks his covenant name, Yahweh, to Moses. While it is unclear whether this is the initial revelation of the name or an exposition of its significance, the name, which is a form of the Hebrew verb "to be," signifies that God defines himself ("I AM WHO I AM," Exod. 3:14).

Upon reaching Egypt, Moses and Aaron encounter resistance from Pharaoh and they display the power of God through a series of signs and plagues. These plagues are considered assaults on the Egyptian gods themselves (12:12), who are depicted as having a limited power exercised by the Egyptian magicians (7:11–13, 22). The biblical text describes these plagues as supernatural intrusions of God's judgment and not natural events. After the death of the firstborn, Pharaoh finally allows the Hebrews to leave Egypt. However, soon after their departure, he changes his mind and pursues them in order to destroy them. God knows Pharaoh's plan, and rather than allowing the Israelites to escape, he actually puts them in a more vulnerable position with their backs against an impassible sea. His purpose is to lure the Egyptians into an attack. When they do attack, God opens the waters of the Red (or Reed) Sea to allow Israel to escape. The waters close on the Egyptian soldiers as an act of judgment. In this way, God displays his glory (14:4, 31), and the Israelites respond with a powerful hymn celebrating God the "warrior" (15:3). The Israelites then set out to Mount Sinai.

Upon their reaching Sinai, God makes his presence known through smoke and fire on the peak of the mountain. Here God delivers his law to the Israelites through Moses. At the apex of the law are the Ten Commandments, given in the form of general ethical principles regulating the relationship between God and humans (commandments 1–4) and between humans (5–10). The case law takes these general ethical principles and applies them to specific situations according to the sociological and redemptive-historical context. An example would be how the goring ox law (21:28–32, 35–36) applies the general ethical principle of the sixth commandment ("You shall not murder") to the case when a person's animal kills a person.

The final part of the book of Exodus describes the construction of the tabernacle, which represents God's abiding presence with his people. This concluding part of the book has three sections. The first section gives instructions for the building (chaps. 25–31), and the last section records the execution of these commands (chaps. 35–40). The importance of this "command-fulfillment" pattern is due to the middle section, the episode of the golden calf (chaps. 32–34). The golden calf story describes how the people, with Aaron's collaboration, substitute the worship of an idol shaped like a calf for the true worship represented by the tabernacle. When Moses returns, he angrily destroys the calf cult with the help of the Levites, who then are "set apart" for special service to God (32:29).

The tabernacle represents God's presence in the Israelite camp. It is his home among the Israelites and thus is a tent, since the Israelites live in tents and at this stage of their history wander from place to place. Even after the Israelites enter the land, the tabernacle will continue to function as the place of worship until they have rest from their enemies, a condition that only comes about with David's defeat of the last enemies of Israel. After this, his son Solomon builds the temple.

God initiates the building of the tabernacle and provides the plans for its construction (25:9, 40; 27:8), the materials for building it (by moving the Egyptian people to giving the Israelites precious items when they left Egypt, 12:36), and even the skill necessary for the building (31:3, 6). The last third of the tabernacle is the Holy of Holies, the place where the ark of the covenant, considered the footstool of God's throne, is placed. The metals used in the construction of the tabernacle increase in preciousness as one moves from the outside area, where bronze is used, toward the Holy of Holies. Bronze gives way to silver and silver to gold. In the Holy of Holies itself, only pure gold is found. In the same way there is restricted access from the outside in. Outside the camp is the realm of Gentiles and ritually unclean Israelites, while only ritually clean Israelites may be in the camp. Only Levites can work in the tabernacle area, though Israelites may come to offer sacrifices accompanied by the Levites. Only once a year may the high priest enter the Holy of Holies (Lev. 16). All of this points to the presence of the Holy God in the tabernacle. At the end of the building of the tabernacle, God makes his presence known by filling it with a cloud that represents his glory (40:34–36).

Authorship, Date, and Addressees: Who Wrote Exodus, When, and to Whom?

Since Exodus is the second part of the Pentateuch, the issue of the authorship, dating, and audience of this book is treated in the Genesis chapter.

Genre: What Style of Literature Is Exodus?

In large part, the book of Exodus continues the type of narrative presentation of Israel's past that we observe in the book of Genesis. While the Exodus account has obvious theological interests and literary shaping, it is still concerned to report what actually happened in time and space. Indeed, in the case of the exodus event, its theological significance is dependent on its actually having happened. Later, Israel will look back on this event in order to gain confidence in a troubled present. In Psalm 77, for instance, the psalmist experiences trouble beyond human help, but at the end of his prayer he gains confidence and hope based on the fact that the exodus, and in particular the crossing of the sea, shows that God can save in such circumstances. Thus, if God did not actually save his people at the sea, the psalmist's confidence is misplaced. In other words, the exodus event establishes a track record for God that Israel later comes to rely on.

The date and exact historical context of the exodus are much debated. The book does not give the names of the Egyptian pharaohs involved in the story, thus making it hard to be dogmatic about the time period. Outside the book of Exodus, the most important passage for identifying the time period is 1 Kings 6:1, which states that Solomon began to build the temple in his fourth year — which was "in the four hundred and eightieth year after the Israelites came out of Egypt." The fourth year of Solomon's reign is 966 BC, and adding 480 years places the exodus in the middle of the fifteenth century BC, a date held by many conservative scholars today. However, many point to problems with this date. While the Pharaoh is not named, one of the store cities that Israel was forced to build was Rameses, a name associated with a long-reigning king of Egypt in the thirteenth century BC. Indeed, the archaeology of the site associated with Rameses (Qantir, Tel el-Daba'a) shows that it was built in the thirteenth century and was not occupied before this time. In addition, the archaeological interpretation of sites associated with the conquest work better with a thirteenth-century date of the exodus (see Joshua chapter). Advocates of the early date argue that the archaeological material can and should be reinterpreted in a way that conforms to the earlier date. This debate continues among scholars who believe that the exodus actually happened. A number of scholars have questioned whether the exodus happened at all, but such a view is the result of a low view of the Bible as a historical testimony in itself.

The book of Exodus also introduces law as a genre. The law expresses God's will for Israel's behavior, beginning with the Ten Commandments and then continuing with the case law. The Ten Commandments express general ethical principles that are applied to specific situations by the case law. The case laws often include penalties for infractions.

Connections: How Does Exodus Anticipate the Gospel?

Each of the three sections of Exodus provides important trajectories into the New Testament and anticipates the coming of Jesus Christ.

The exodus event (chaps. 1–18) is the most important salvation event in the Old Testament. Later prophets announce a coming judgment due to Israel's unrepentant sin. But after the judgment, they proclaim a restoration of relationship and often speak of this restoration as a "second exodus." This exodus, too, will involve a return via the wilderness:

A voice of one calling:
"In the wilderness prepare
    the way for the LORD;
make straight in the desert
    a highway for our God . . ."
(Isa. 40:3; see also 35:5–10; 43:13–21; Hos. 2:14–16).

Mark announces that Jesus Christ is the ultimate fulfillment of this expectation by quoting these verses at the head of his gospel

(Mark 1:2 – 3). All the Gospels demonstrate that Jesus is the fulfillment of the exodus by drawing our attention to the parallels between his life and ministry. To name a few, after being baptized in the Jordan River (comparable to Israel's crossing of the sea [cf. 1 Cor. 10:1 – 6], where Paul says that the Israelites were baptized in the sea), Jesus goes into the wilderness for forty days and forty nights and experiences three temptations that Israel experienced in the wilderness (Matt. 4:1 – 11). Unlike Israel, which succumbed to the temptations, Jesus resists them by citing Deuteronomy — the book recording Moses' final sermon to the wilderness generation — three times. Jesus is the obedient Son of God in contrast to the Israelites. According to Matthew (see chaps. 5 – 7), Jesus then goes to a mountain, where he delivers a sermon on the subject of the law. No one familiar with the Old Testament can miss the parallel with the book of Exodus, where Yahweh delivers the law on Mount Sinai.

The most dramatic parallel between Jesus' life and work and the exodus occurs in connection with his crucifixion, which takes place on the Passover, the annual celebration of the release from Egypt (Exodus 12:1 – 30). Jesus is the Passover lamb (1 Cor. 5:7). The exodus is the shadow of which Jesus is the reality.

The connection of the law with the New Testament is a complex issue, but we should begin with Jesus' strong affirmation of the Old Testament law in Matthew 5:17 – 20. Of course, Jesus fulfills the law in a way that means, as the New Testament clearly indicates, that some of the rules are no longer to be observed (the ceremonial laws and laws concerning ritual purity). The moral law, both in the Ten Commandments and in the case law, retains its relevance. However, one did not enter into a relationship with God through observance of the law, during either the Old or the New Testament periods, and Paul spoke harshly about those who taught that law is the basis for the divine-human relationship. Nevertheless, the law, then and now, expresses God's will for how people should live and thus maintain their relationship with him. No one can keep the law perfectly, except Christ. He keeps the law in our place and suffers the penalty of the law on our behalf. Jesus is the divine lawgiver and law keeper and the one who suffers the penalty of the law.

Finally, the tabernacle also anticipates Christ. The tabernacle represents God's presence among his people during the period between the time of Moses and David. After all, Jesus himself is God and thus represents his presence: "The Word became flesh and made his dwelling among us" (John 1:14). The connection of this verse to the ancient tabernacle is seen when it is recognized that the verb translated "made his dwelling" comes from the Greek *skenao*, which is related to the noun *skene*, "tabernacle." A more literal translation would be "The Word became flesh and tabernacled among us."

Recommended Resources

Enns, P. *Exodus*. NIVAC. Grand Rapids: Zondervan, 2000.

Hoffmeier, J. K. *Israel in Egypt: The Evidence for the Authenticity of the Exodus Tradition*. Oxford: Oxford University Press, 1997.

Longman, T. *How to Read Exodus*. Downers Grove, IL: InterVarsity Press, 2009.

Wells, B. "Exodus." Pages 160–283 in ZIBBC 1. Edited by J. H. Walton. Grand Rapids: Zondervan, 2009.

Questions for Review and Discussion

1. How does the exodus event, and in particular the crossing of the sea, demonstrate God's glory (Exod. 14:4, 31)?
2. What is the relationship between the Ten Commandments and the case law? Give examples.
3. How does the tabernacle represent God's presence?
4. Is the historicity of the exodus event important? Why or why not?
5. How do the Gospel stories relate Jesus to the exodus? What significance does such a connection have?

chapter four

THE BOOK
OF LEVITICUS

Content: What Is Leviticus About?

Leviticus means "matters pertaining to the Levites," since much of
the book concerns subjects of interest to the priests of Israel.

Leviticus 1–7: Sacrifices

Sacrifices constitute the first subject of the book (chaps. 1–7). Five
sacrifices are described with an emphasis on how to perform the
ritual, with little explication of the significance of the ritual, though
often we can surmise what is meant by the various actions undertaken.

The "burnt offering" (*'ola*) is a sacrifice that offers atonement
for sin (chap. 1; 6:8–13). The animal is killed and totally consumed
by the fire, since it represents the sinner who needs to restore his
relationship with God. The worshiper identifies with the animal
by laying his hands on its head before it is killed (1:4). Instructions
are given as to whether the animal is from the herd (vv. 3–9), from
the flock (vv. 10–13), or a bird (vv. 14–17). The type of offering is
dependent on the ability of the worshiper to pay for the animal.

The second offering is called a "grain offering" (chap. 2;
6:14–23), although the Hebrew term (*minha*) means gift or tribute.
The grain may be uncooked or cooked in various forms. A portion
of the grain is taken and mixed with incense and burned as a gift to
God. The rest is given to the priests. The instructions specify that
yeast and (fruit) honey are not to be added to the sacrifice (2:11),
probably because when it burns, it ferments—a form of decay. On
the other hand, salt is always to be added in order to represent the

covenant (2:13), probably because the salt survives the fire, the way the covenant persists through the difficulties of life.

The third sacrifice is the "fellowship offering" (chap. 3; 7:11 – 21) — sometimes translated "peace offering," since the word is related to the Hebrew word for peace (*shelamim*). As opposed to the burnt offering, only a part of the animal is burned on the altar to God. The rest is enjoyed by the worshipers themselves in the context of fellowship.

The last two sacrifices are specific atonement sacrifices, the sin offering (*hattat*; 4:1 – 5:13; 6:24 – 30) and the guilt offering (*asham*; 5:14 – 6:7; 7:1 – 10). The exact condition as to when these sacrifices were offered is unclear to us. The sin offering, however, is connected in large part to infractions of ritual purity and therefore is sometimes understood to be a purification ritual. The guilt offering involves a violation of "any of the LORD's holy things" (5:15). It also appears that one is able to put a monetary valuation on the sin, since restitution is called for plus a penalty of 20 percent. For this reason, the sacrifice is sometimes called a reparation offering.

Leviticus 8 – 10: The Priests

Aaron and his sons are set apart for service in the holy place. They are given priestly garments and are anointed with oil in order to identify them with the tabernacle and set them apart to be in the presence of God. They offer sacrifices to atone for their sins. This section also includes the tragic story of Aaron's sons, who offer "unauthorized" (10:1) fire before the Lord. God responds by consuming them with fire, thus serving as a warning of the dangers of the priesthood.

Leviticus 11 – 16: Laws concerning Ritual Purity

A major concern of the laws of Leviticus has to do with ritual purity or cleanness. Food (chap. 11), childbirth (chap. 12), skin diseases and mildew (chaps. 13 – 14), and bodily fluids (chap. 15) are the main topics.

In order to fully participate in the life of Israel, including visiting the holy place, an Israelite had to be ritually pure. Exactly what distinguishes clean from unclean is not always absolutely clear. Even so, we can observe certain principles at work, including an emphasis on creation order, wholeness, and life/death. In terms of creation order, it seems that kosher (or "clean") animals and fish conform to the norms of creation. A lobster, for instance, is not clean, because it does not have the expected fins and scales (11:9). The birds that are considered unclean (11:13–19) are all carrion birds and thus associated with death. Moreover, the law announces that anyone who has skin disease is considered unclean unless the skin disease covers the person from head to foot (13:12–17). The underlying principle is not health, but wholeness. Blood and semen connected to the reproductive system render a person unclean because they are fluids associated with life and thus holy. Coming into contact with something holy has the effect of rendering a person unclean.

The last chapter of this section (chap. 16) details the ritual of the Day of Atonement. This day is the only time anyone can enter the Holy of Holies, and it can only be the high priest, for the purpose of purifying the holy place from the accumulated sins of the past year. These sins are seen as being carried off by the scapegoat that is driven out into the wilderness (16:10).

Leviticus 17–27: The Holiness Code

The final section of Leviticus is a separate collection of laws that are bound together by the concern to urge Israel to be holy ("set apart" or "consecrated"). Indeed, the call to be holy is repeated in several places in this collection (19:2; 20:7, 26; 21:6; 23:20). While most of this section is directed to all of Israel, priestly regulations are found in chapters 21–22 and 24.

Authorship and Date: Who Wrote Leviticus and When?

For the most part, since Leviticus is part three of the Pentateuch, this issue has been dealt with in the chapter on Genesis. There is a question as to whether the Holiness Code (chaps. 17–27) was originally a separate composition, but deciding this issue is not important for interpretation.

Genre: What Style of Literature Is Leviticus?

Law constitutes the largest part of the book of Leviticus (see description in the chapter on Exodus), though there is some historical narrative as well (chaps. 8–10; see also the Excursus on Theological History).

Connections: How Does Leviticus Anticipate the Gospel?

Leviticus provides a rich and profound background for the gospel story. Jesus is the ultimate sacrifice anticipated by the animal sacrifices of the Old Testament. Since he is the once-and-for-all sacrifice (Heb. 10:1 – 18), Christians do not offer animal sacrifices. He is also the ultimate priest, although this is communicated by the book of Hebrews by comparing him to Melchizedek (Gen. 14:18 – 20), who is considered superior to Aaron (Heb. 4:14 – 5:10; 7:1 – 8:13). The laws of ritual purity are not relevant today. They served the purpose of differentiating Israelites/Jews from Gentiles, and now that the wall of hostility between these two groups has been torn down due to the work of Christ (Eph. 2:14 – 18), the food laws (Acts 10) and the other ritual purity laws are no longer observed.

Recommended Resources

Gane, R. *Leviticus, Numbers*. NIVAC. Grand Rapids: Zondervan, 2004.

_____. "Leviticus." Pages 284 – 337 in ZIBBC 1. Edited by J. H. Walton. Grand Rapids: Zondervan, 2009.

Hartley, J. E. *Leviticus*. WBC. Nashville: Word, 1992.

Hess, R. S. "Leviticus." Pages 565 – 826 in *Genesis – Leviticus*. EBC-R 1. Edited by T. Longman and D. E. Garland. Grand Rapids: Zondervan, 2008.

Longman, T. *Immanuel in Our Place: Seeing Christ in Israel's Worship*. Phillipsburg, NJ: P and R Publishing, 2001.

Questions for Review and Discussion

1. What purpose did sacrifices serve in Israel? What relevance do they have for Christian readers?
2. What function(s) did priests serve during the time of the Old Testament? Are there priests today? Why or why not?
3. Why were Israelites to observe the Day of Atonement?
4. Why don't Christians worry about ritual purity?

chapter five

THE BOOK
OF NUMBERS

Content: What Is Numbers About?

Numbers is part four of the five-part Pentateuch, explaining why the Israelites had to spend forty years in the wilderness and narrating the vast bulk of that time period. The book also describes the transition from the first generation, who left Egypt, to the second generation, who will enter the Promised Land.

Numbers can be outlined according to the geographical setting of the different parts of the book. At first (1:1 – 10:10) the Israelites are in the camp in the Sinai wilderness, where they have been since Exodus 19. In the second section (10:11 – 20:13) they are in the region around Kadesh, and then finally (20:14 – 36:13) they move from Kadesh to the plains of Moab (22:1; 36:13), which will be the setting for the book of Deuteronomy. However, an even more interesting but looser structure may be observed by noting two key chapters, 1 and 26, both of which present a census of military personnel (and likely suggested the name "Numbers" for the book). The first counts the men who left Egypt, and the second counts the second generation, the now-adult offspring of the exodus generation. These two censuses — or better, military registrations — mark an important transition that is a major theme of the book: the shift from the first generation of judgment to the second generation of hope.

Thus, chapters 1 – 25 focus on the first generation. Numbers 1:1 – 10:10, which as we have seen takes place at the camp in the Sinai wilderness, narrates the preparation for the march. After the counting of the fighting men, chapter 2 describes the layout of the wilderness camp, which looks like an ancient Near Eastern army camp. Israel is an army on the march. (Note Moses' call to march in 10:35.) Job descriptions are given for the various clans of Levites (chaps. 3–4), and additional laws are enumerated (chaps. 5–6). Numbers 7:1–10:9 majors in matters concerning the tabernacle.

Once the march is under way, most of the stories concern the sins of and judgments on the first generation. Lay and priestly leaders rebel against Moses, God's appointed leader (chaps. 12; 16–17). The people constantly complain about God's provision (e.g., chap. 11). In chapters 13–14 we learn that the twelve spies return with a positive report about the bounty of the Promised Land; however, all but two (Joshua and Caleb) believe that the Israelites cannot dislodge the formidable natives. This lack of confidence in God is the straw that breaks the camel's back, and God decrees that the first generation will die in the wilderness (with the exception of the two faithful spies). Moses and Aaron disqualify themselves from entering the land when they attribute to themselves the provision of water from the rock and beat it with a stick rather than speak to it as God commanded (20:1–13).

Even so, God continues to be with his people as they march through the wilderness, as demonstrated by the episode with Balaam, the foreign prophet hired by the king of Moab to curse Israel. God allowed Balaam only to bless them. Even so, Israel continued to rebel against God, since many of the men slept with Midianite women, a plot hatched by Balaam (31:16). Interestingly, a plaster inscription written in black and red ink discovered during excavations at Deir 'Alla in Jordan mentions Balaam and calls him a "seer of the gods." This inscription is dated to the mid-eighth to seventh century BC, which is some centuries after the time of the wilderness wanderings; but it does establish knowledge of Balaam's non-Israelite priest in a non-Israelite setting.

The story of the failure of the first generation ends in chapter 25, and the remainder of the book follows the second generation, whose census is found in chapter 26. As such, the rest of Numbers presents positive stories of military victory (chap. 31) and preparations for the entrance into the land. When the book ends, the people are poised on the plains of Moab, across from Jericho (36:13). They will cross into the Promised Land from this point, but not before Moses preaches to them (see chapter on Deuteronomy).

Authorship and Date: Who Wrote Numbers and When?

The major issues of the authorship and date of writing of Numbers, part four of the Pentateuch, are treated in the chapter on Genesis.

Genre: What Style of Literature Is Numbers?

Like Exodus and Leviticus, Numbers continues the theological history of the wanderings in the wilderness in combination with law (see the Excursus on Theological History).

Connections: How Does Numbers Anticipate the Gospel?

God stays involved with his rebellious people in the book of Numbers, working for their redemption and restoration. Even though he punishes them, he does not reject them. The New Testament continues this theme. Indeed, the New Testament is its climax. The Old Testament is simply a prelude to what happens on the Cross. God's people continued to turn against him, yet he nevertheless sent his Son, Jesus Christ, whom they treated brutally (Mark 12:1 – 12). God did not abandon his people, but provided hope for them in the salvation offered by Jesus Christ. Each generation of Christians should place themselves in the position of the new generation of the book of Numbers. God has acted redemptively in our midst, and by so doing, he has given our lives meaning and hope. Just like the Numbers generation, we are called upon to respond to God's grace with obedience.

Recommended Resources

Cole, R. D. *Numbers*. NAC. Nashville: Broadman & Holman, 2001.
_____. "Numbers." Pages 338 – 417 in ZIBBC 1. Edited by J. H. Walton. Grand Rapids: Zondervan, 2009.

Gane, R. *Leviticus, Numbers*. NIVAC. Grand Rapids: Zondervan, 2004.

Olson, D. T. *Numbers*. Interp. Louisville, KY: Westminster John Knox, 1996.
_____. *The Death of the Old and the Birth of the New: The Framework of the Book of Numbers and the Pentateuch*. BJS 71. Chico, CA: Scholars Press, 1985.

Questions for Review and Discussion

1. What period of time does Numbers encompass?
2. What is the relationship between Numbers 1 and 26, and how do they relate to the major theme of the book?
3. What is the importance of the spy narrative (chaps. 13–14) to the message of the book?

chapter six

THE BOOK
OF DEUTERONOMY

Content: What Is Deuteronomy About?

Deuteronomy means "second law" and underlines the fact that the book replicates in many ways the giving of the law at Mount Sinai as found in Exodus 19–24. Forty years after the giving of the law, Moses is preaching to the second generation of the people of Israel — born in the wilderness and ready to enter the Promised Land — on the plains of Moab across the Jordan River. Moses admonishes them by telling them not to disobey as their fathers did, who died in the wilderness.

Moses' sermon takes the form of a covenant-treaty document because he is leading Israel in a reaffirmation of the covenant just before his death. The text introduces God and Israel, the two covenant partners, with Moses as the mediator of the relationship (1:1–5). After the introduction comes the historical prologue, the purpose of which is to outline the relationship between the covenant partners up until the present (1:9–3:29). Following the historical summary, Moses speaks of God's law, his will for how his covenant people will live before him (chaps. 4–26). He repeats the Ten Commandments (5:6–21) and enumerates many case laws that are applications of the principles of the Ten Commandments to specific situations according to the sociological and redemptive-historical context of the people of God at the time.

The next section of the book specifies rewards and punishments (chaps. 27–28). If people keep the law, they will experience blessings such as wealth, peace, success, happy families. But if they do not keep the law, great punishments will follow: defeat, hunger, and death.

As a legal document, the text names witnesses who will monitor the observance of the agreement between the parties (30:19) in the context of calling on Israel to make a choice to affirm the covenant (30:11–20). There is also the provision to reaffirm the covenant every seven years by rereading the law in front of all the people (31:9–13).

While the foregoing is a summary of the contents of the book of Deuteronomy, it is helpful to highlight certain distinctive laws that will play a large role in later biblical books.

The first, relevant to Joshua as well as other biblical books, are the laws of warfare (chaps. 7 and 20). These laws make a distinction between warfare inside and outside of Israel. Outside of Israel, after defeating an enemy, the Israelites must kill every male but spare the women and children. Inside of Israel, everything must be subjected to *herem*—that is, all the plunder must be given to God and everyone must be killed. This regulation was to keep Israel from being religiously contaminated by the local pagan population (7:1–6; 20:16–18).

The second law, influential in later books—particularly Kings (thus the next two laws)—is the law of centralization (chap. 12). Looking into the future when God gives Israel rest from its internal enemies, it envisions a time when God will choose a place to make his presence known. After he does so, it will be the only place where sacrificial worship will be legitimate. All other worship will be considered inappropriate and punishable.

The third law is the law of the king (17:14–20). The king must be pious, constantly studying God's law as well as avoiding the wicked behavior of most foreign monarchs that would show a lack of confidence in God. These behaviors include taking a large harem (often denoting political alliances with foreign states), amassing wealth, or assembling a formidable army.

Finally, it is important to remember that the laws of the prophets will play an important role in the book of Kings as well as in the development of the institution of prophecy. These laws complement each other as they help Israelites to differentiate between a true prophet and a false prophet. The first law (13:1–5) tells Israel that a true prophet will always speak in the name of Yahweh, so any prophet who speaks in the name of another god is a false prophet even if his prophecy comes true. The second law (18:14–22) proclaims that a prophet is false if he speaks in the name of the true God, but his prophecy does not come true.

Authorship and Date: Who Wrote Deuteronomy and When?

Since Deuteronomy is the fifth and final installment of the literary body known as the Torah or Pentateuch, issues concerning authorship and date may be found in the chapter on Genesis. However, Deuteronomy offers some interesting additional issues. It presents itself as a sermon by Moses, yet his speech is contained within the context of third-person omniscient narrative. Thus the book, like the rest of the Pentateuch, is anonymous, even though the speeches are represented as coming from Moses himself. Conservative commentators take this at face value and place the Moses speeches at the time of Moses (either the fifteenth or thirteenth century BC). That said, not all, but many of these interpreters also recognize post-Mosaic additions to the book—and not only an obvious one such as the account of Moses' death (chap. 34). For instance, there is a narrative voice in the book that is clearly post-Mosaic, since it describes events "east of the Jordan" (1:1, 5; 3:8, etc.)—meaning the Transjordan— even though it is clear that Moses never came to the Cisjordan so that the Transjordan was "across the river" from him.

Thus it seems reasonable that although the book of Deuteronomy originated in a sermon that Moses gave to Israel on the eve of his death in order to lead them in a covenant reaffirmation, the book also contains considerable post-Mosaic additions and redaction and may not have reached final form until the end of the Old Testament time period.

Genre: What Style of Literature Is Deuteronomy?

The book of Deuteronomy presents Moses' final sermon, an exhortation to the people whom he has led for over four decades. The central message of the sermon is to encourage God's people to keep his law. Moses is speaking to the second generation born in the wilderness. Their parents died in the wilderness because of their sin, so Moses wants to impress on them the importance of following God's law. Thus the book repeats the Ten Commandments (5:6–21) and even more fully develops the case law that applies the principles of the commandments to specific situations (chaps. 6–26). The case law is an exposition of the Ten Commandments (see also the chapter on Exodus).

Indeed, the structure of Moses' sermon is that of a covenant-treaty document. Moses calls on Israel to renew the covenant commitment it made to God at Mount Sinai (Exod. 19–24), often called the Mosaic or Sinaitic covenant. Earlier we saw how the different parts of the book of Deuteronomy follow the structure of a covenant-treaty document. Experts in the study of ancient Near Eastern literature have shown how this structure follows the outline of Hittite and Assyrian treaties, helping modern readers to understand that a covenant is like a treaty between two nations.

Connections: How Does Deuteronomy Anticipate the Gospel?

Rather than focusing on specific examples, we will draw attention to how Deuteronomy as a whole anticipates the New Testament. The book is a covenant-treaty renewal document. Moses is leading the people in a reaffirmation of the covenant made at Sinai (Exod. 19–24). Thus the book as a whole fits into a biblical theology of covenant that culminates in the New Testament.

The first time a covenant is mentioned in the Bible is in connection with Noah (Gen. 6:8; 9:9–17). After the flood, God made a covenant with Noah and the whole of creation assuring the continuance of the world and its regular seasons. The rainbow was the sign of this covenant (9:12–13). Now, it is surprising that the first mention of a covenant comes in the Noah story, but theologians have commented that even though the word is not used, it is appropriate to speak of a covenant with Adam. After all, there was a law (not to eat of the fruit of "the tree of the knowledge of good and evil," Gen. 2:17) with an understood punishment for transgression — namely, death. The fact that there are a number of verbal echoes between Genesis 2 and 9 also signals a connection between these texts. If this viewpoint is correct, then it may be better to speak of the Adamic covenant as a covenant of creation and the Noahic covenant as one of re-creation.

In any case, there is no doubt about the fact that the next covenant in the Bible is between God and Abraham. This covenant emphasizes promises — the promises that Abraham's descendants will become a great nation, implying land and people, and that they will be blessed and a blessing to the nations (Gen. 12:1–3). While, again, the term "covenant" is not used in this immediate context, the relationship is spoken of as a covenant on those occasions when God came back to renew his promises to Abraham (15:18; 17:2). The sign of this covenant was circumcision (17:9–14).

The next covenant is the one made with Israel through Moses at Mount Sinai, a covenant that emphasizes law (Exod. 19–24). We have seen how Deuteronomy is a renewal of this covenant. Other renewals are reported elsewhere in the Old Testament (Josh. 24; 1 Sam. 12; Neh. 8–10). The sign of the Mosaic covenant was the Sabbath (Exod. 31:12–18).

The final Old Testament covenant is the one made with David. God chooses David to be king over Israel and confirms with him that there will be a descendant of his on the throne forever (2 Sam. 7; 1 Chron. 17). There is no specific sign associated with this covenant.

While the Davidic covenant of kingship is the final Old Testament covenant, Jeremiah 31:31–34 provides an important transitional statement between the Old Testament and the New Testament. The people of Israel have not been able to keep the Old Testament covenant, as witnessed by their frequent sins and God's necessary judgment. But Jeremiah looks beyond the judgment he has announced and sees a restoration of God's people, one that will result in a "new covenant." Jeremiah describes this new covenant as being more intense, more intimate, more internal, and more immediate than the old covenant.

The New Testament announces that the new covenant has come to fulfillment in the work of Jesus Christ (Luke 22:20; Heb. 8). Jesus establishes the new covenant, and its sign is the sacrament of the Lord's Supper. Jesus' new covenant does not just replace the old covenant but actually fulfills it. He fulfills the Davidic covenant because he is the king (the Christ, or Messiah) who is David's son who rules forever on the throne. He fulfills the Mosaic covenant of law as the perfect keeper of the law and paradoxically as the one who suffers the penalties of the law on our behalf. He fulfills the Abrahamic covenant, according to Paul, because he is the "seed" promised to Abraham (Gal. 3:16). The manner in which he fulfills the Adamic-Noahic covenant of creation is likely to be found in Paul's argument that he is the "second Adam" (Rom. 5:12–21). In a word, Jesus Christ brings to culmination the covenants of the Old Testament, of which Deuteronomy is a prime example.

Recommended Resources

Carpenter, E. E. "Deuteronomy." Pages 418–547 in ZIBBC 1. Edited by J. H. Walton. Grand Rapids: Zondervan, 2009.

Kline, M. G. *Treaty of the Great King*. Grand Rapids: Eerdmans, 1963.

McConville, J. *Deuteronomy*. Apollos. Leicester, UK: Inter-Varsity Press, 2002.

Questions for Review and Discussion

1. What does the name "Deuteronomy" mean, and how does that name reflect the contents of the book?
2. What are some of the laws of Deuteronomy that exert a strong influence on later Scripture?
3. List the implications of the treaty nature of the covenant.
4. What role do witnesses play in the book?
5. What role does covenant play in the developing theology of the Old and New Testaments?

chapter seven

THE BOOK OF JOSHUA

Content: What Is Joshua About?

The Pentateuch ended with a cliffhanger that expects a sequel. Deuteronomy records the final sermon Moses gives to Israel before they enter the land and in anticipation of their entry into the land. The last chapter describes Moses ascending Mount Nebo, the place where he will die, and so the assumption is that Joshua inherits the leadership of Israel as they stand poised to enter the land.

Joshua picks up the action where Deuteronomy leaves off. The first part of the book describes Israel's violent entry into the land (chaps. 1–12), while the second part narrates the distribution of the conquered land to the various tribes as well as Joshua's parting words to the Israelites (chaps. 13–24).

Before Israel engages the Canaanites in battle, they prepare for the war (1:1–6:27) according to the law of warfare (Deut. 7 and 20). In chapter 1 God assures Joshua that he will be with him as he was with Moses, on condition that he will observe the law that God gave to Moses, a condition that Joshua affirms. Joshua sends spies into Canaan, and they are assisted by Rahab, a Canaanite prostitute, who affirms Yahweh's power and thus is incorporated into Israel along with her family (chap. 2). Rahab's story reveals that it was possible for some Canaanites to avoid being killed and to join Israel. Israel then crosses into the Promised Land, led by priests who carry the ark of the covenant (chap. 3). As the priests' feet touch the waters of the Jordan River, the waters stop flowing, so they enter the land on dry ground, a reactualization of the miracle at the Red (Reed) Sea, showing that the God who defeated Egypt is still with them as they face an even greater enemy. Once they cross into the Promised Land, the Israelites perform certain rituals to spiritually prepare for the battle. First, the men, who apparently had not been circumcised at birth in the wilderness, are circumcised—a dangerous move, since the operation would physically weaken them in the neighborhood of their enemies in Jericho (see Gen. 34). Second, they observe the Passover. While dangerous, it is necessary for the fighting men to spiritually prepare themselves for battle, and they need to be as ritually pure as possible in order to enter the precincts of the sanctuary. After all, God the Divine Warrior is on the battlefield with the army of Israel.

That God is present with Israel in battle is made clear when Joshua encounters God himself in the guise of a warrior (5:13–15). In this meeting, Joshua gets his marching orders against Jericho. Jericho is presented as a formidable city with massive defensive walls. Even so, Jericho falls to the Israelites easily because the people obey the instructions God gave them. This battle report contrasts dramatically with the next one concerning the city of Ai (7:1–8:29). While Jericho is a well-fortified city, Ai is not. Indeed, the name Ai means "dump" or "trash heap." However, when Joshua sends his army to take Ai, it is roundly defeated. In response to Joshua's lament, God informs him that the defeat was due to an infraction of the laws concerning holy war, specifically the theft of the war plunder that was supposed to be turned over to the Lord and not kept for individual profit. Once the culprit, Achan, is exposed and executed, then Israel does defeat the town. After this second victory and while the Israelites are in their war camp in Gilgal, an embassy of foreigners approaches Joshua and requests a treaty (chap. 9). They look as if they have come from afar, and Joshua agrees to a treaty, but without making inquiry of God (9:14). As it turns out, the embassy is not from far away or outside the land, but from Ai just down the road. God had forbidden Israel from making treaties with people in the land (Deut. 20:15–18), but now they are committed. Joshua's rash agreement will later haunt Israel (2 Sam. 21:1–14).

The accounts of Jericho, Ai, and Gibeon are given in such detail in order to be a lesson to Israel later on. These three episodes illustrate the consequences of obedience (victory; Jericho), the consequences of disobedience (defeat; Ai), and the complication that results from not seeking God's will in a matter (Gibeon).

Even so, by the end of chapter 9, Israel now controls the central part of the Promised Land. The Canaanite kings of the south then band together and attack Gibeon, an act that brings Israel into the conflict since they are now in treaty relationship with Gibeon (chap. 10). While it is to Israel's advantage that these southern kings take to the open battlefield rather than staying behind their walled cities, it does not mean, even though they defeat the kings with God's help, that they will actually occupy their cities. The same is true of the northern kingdom, which also takes to the battlefield once the southern coalition is defeated (chap. 11). Joshua 12 presents a summary statement concerning the defeat of Canaan, with an emphasis on the victories and no mention of the land that still is not under Israelite control.

Most of the second part of the book of Joshua (chaps. 13–22) describes the distribution of the land to the Israelite tribes. That God is in control of the parceling out of the land is made clear by the fact that the distribution is performed by the priest who casts the divine lots. While the emphasis in chapters 1–12 is on victory, the second half of the book makes it clear that not all the land is yet controlled by Israel. All the tribes receive their inheritance. Simeon and Levi, however, do not get separate land allotments but rather cities within the territory of other tribes as anticipated by Jacob's curse on them (Gen. 49:5–8). Even so, the emphasis throughout is that the ancient promise of land given to Abraham (Gen. 12:1–3) is finally being fulfilled.

The last two chapters of the book (23–24) concern Joshua's farewell. The final chapter is a covenant renewal ceremony reminiscent of the book of Deuteronomy, which served that purpose before Moses' death. The people do indeed swear to follow God after Joshua's death, a commitment betrayed according to the book of Judges.

Authorship and Date: Who Wrote Joshua and When?

The book of Joshua is anonymous; thus the authorship and exact date are unknown. While early tradition assigns the book to Joshua himself, there are indications that the book, at least in its final form, was written well after the events it narrates. One of the surest signs of this is the frequent use of the phrase "to this day," which requires that some time has passed since the events that are narrated in the book (4:9; 5:9; 6:25; 7:26; 8:28–29; 9:27; 10:27; 13:13; 15:63; 16:10). Because the book exhibits a perspective similar to that of the author of the book of Samuel-Kings, it is possible that Joshua received its final form at the same time as those books, namely, the exilic period (586 – 539 BC).

Genre: What Style of Literature Is Joshua?

Joshua presents itself as a work of history. That is, the book describes events that happened in space and time in the past. As with all works of history, the book presents a selective and interpretive account of events. Its perspective is driven by what it considers important, and since the narrative makes it clear that the composer(s) of the book felt that God's actions in the events were most important and worthy of highlighting, it is accurate to describe Joshua as a theological history.

That Joshua is a work of history does not necessarily imply that everything is presented accurately. Indeed, the reliability of Joshua's rendering of the conquest and settlement is the subject of much discussion, raising the question, is Joshua historically accurate?

Joshua presents a picture of Israel entering into Canaan from Egypt and taking the land by means of warfare. This description is greeted by skepticism by many today on two grounds. First, the very optimistic portrayal of Israel's defeat of Canaan in chapters 1 – 12 seems at odds with the acknowledgment of key land still controlled by Canaanites in Joshua 13 – 22 and Judges 1. Second, archaeological research in Egypt (as in the store city of Rameses) and Israel does not seem to support the biblical depiction. Many of the details of this issue are raised in the chapter on Exodus, whose historicity is closely bound up with the issue of the conquest.

Thus, rather than rehearsing the details of the problems, here we will simply describe some of the leading alternative theories for how the Israelites came into the land.

(1) The Immigration Model: In the light of the lack of destruction layers in the archaeological records of cities mentioned in the Conquest narratives, some have argued that Israel came and peacefully settled in the hinterlands between the great Canaanite cities. Once the latter began to crumble (for reasons that are unclear), the Israelites began to take over the land. Due to a lack of support in ancient texts as well as the absence of an explanation for how a peaceful immigration could lead to the takeover of the land, few if any hold this view today.

(2) The Revolution Model: Taking cues from the story of Rahab (Josh. 2), reading between the lines of the Amarna tablets (letters from the city rulers of Canaan to the Egyptian pharaoh dating to the four-

teenth century BC), and mixing in a healthy dose of Marxist sociological theory, some have come to believe that what we know of as Israel found its origins in the underclasses of Canaanites who successfully revolted against their feudal overlords. For many, the idea of an ancient revolution of the proletariat is too modern an explanation of the ancient text.

(3) The Internal Transformation Model: In what is perhaps the most popular alternative model today, modern archaeologists note the sudden appearance of hundreds of small central hill-country villages at the same time that large Canaanite coastal cities are falling apart (the transition point between the Late Bronze and the Early Iron ages, ca. 1250 BC). These hill-country villages share certain technologies (plaster-lined cisterns; olive grove terracing) as well as pottery and an intriguing absence of pig bones. The supposition of this view is that these hill-country sites are the start of a new society later known as Israel, derived from Canaanite culture.

(4) The Minimalists: This last perspective is not really an alternative model, but rather a radically skeptical conclusion. Since the biblical text is ideologically biased, these scholars reason, we cannot reconstruct history using its contents. Since, in their opinion at least, archaeology does not directly attest to the existence of Israel until much later, not only did the conquest not occur, but also Israel did not come into existence until much, much later.

Rather than arguing against these individual models, it is necessary to see the inadequacy of the reasons for positing them in the first place. The argument that Joshua 1 – 12 (with its emphasis on the positive outcome of the conquest) and Judges 1 (with its acknowledgment that the conquest was incomplete) contradict each other in the matter of the conquest is the result of misunderstanding the intentions of these two sections of Scripture. Joshua 1 – 12 selects positive stories of conquest in order to celebrate the beginning of the fulfillment of the Abrahamic promise of land. It should not be read to claim that every square mile of Canaan was taken by Joshua. After all, two of the key battles were on the open battlefield, not implying that Joshua took over the cities themselves. While it is true that traditional readings of the archaeological record come into conflict with the biblical account of (exodus and) conquest, it is also important to remember that the record can be interpreted in other ways more supportive of the biblical text.

Before concluding, we must also acknowledge that although the Bible presents the conquest by intruders into the land as the core of later Israel, it also allows for the peaceful immigration of some as well as the involvement of Canaanites like Rahab who decide to embrace the worship of Yahweh and make Israel their new people.

Connections: How Does Joshua Anticipate the Gospel?

Joshua depicts God as a warrior fighting on behalf of his people and bringing them victories and initial possession of the land of Canaan. In this way God not only establishes a homeland for his people but brings his judgment against the inhabitants of the land (Gen. 15:16). How does this picture of God as a warrior anticipate the gospel?

To answer this question, we must further develop the Old Testament background to God's warring activity. After all, God also appears as a warrior outside of the narratives of the conquest. Indeed, we see God fighting for the judges of Israel, David, Jehoshaphat, and many others. But we also see God fighting *against* Israel. In the book of Joshua, God fights against Israel when it disobeys the rules of warfare (at Ai, chap. 7). Perhaps the most dramatic description of God's warfare against disobedient Israel may be seen in Lamentations 2, which poetically describes God coming against Jerusalem "as an enemy" at the time of the Babylonian attack. Finally, although the Old Testament ends with Israel living under foreign oppression, the prophets announce that God will come again as warrior in order to deliver Israel from its enemies (Dan. 7; Zech. 14; Mal. 4).

When the New Testament begins, we hear the voice of John the Baptist, who speaks similarly to those Old Testament prophets. He pronounces violent judgment on the wicked, chopping them with an ax like rotten wood (Matt. 3:10) and burning them with fire like chaff (3:11–12). When Jesus begins his ministry, he does not seem to act on the promise of the prophets and John. Rather, he heals the sick, exorcises demons, and preaches the Good News. While this raises questions in John's mind (Matt. 11:3), Jesus responds in a way that tells him that he is the Divine Warrior, though his warfare is not against flesh-and-blood enemies, but against the spiritual powers and authorities. This battle is not won with spears and swords, but with spiritual weapons and indeed ultimately by Christ's death, resurrection, and ascension (Matt. 26:52–56; Eph. 4:7–8; 6:10–20; Col. 2:13–15).

Even so, John the Baptist was not wrong in envisioning the warring Messiah as bringing a violent end to evil. As a prophet, however, he did not understand the timing. Jesus is coming again. The apocalyptic portions of the New Testament (particularly Matt. 24; Mark 13; Luke 21; Revelation) picture the return of the warrior, who will bring to an end all human and spiritual evil (see, for instance, Rev. 19:11–21). In an important way, the stories of conquest in Joshua provide a preview and warning concerning the final judgment.

Recommended Resources

Gundry, S., ed. *Show Them No Mercy: Four Views on God and the Canaanite Genocide.* Grand Rapids: Zondervan, 2003.

Hess, R. S. *Joshua.* TOTC. Downers Grove, IL: InterVarsity Press, 1996.

_____. "Joshua." Pages 2–93 in ZIBBC 2. Edited by J. H. Walton. Grand Rapids: Zondervan, 2009.

Longman, T., and D. Reid. *God Is a Warrior.* Grand Rapids: Zondervan, 1995.

Provan, I., V. P. Long, and T. Longman. *A Biblical History of Israel.* Louisville, KY: Westminster John Knox, 2003.

Woudstra, M. *The Book of Joshua.* NICOT. Grand Rapids: Eerdmans, 1981.

Questions for Review and Discussion

1. How does Joshua relate to the end of the book of Deuteronomy?
2. Summarize the contents of the two major parts of Joshua.
3. Why were the Israelites circumcised, and why did they celebrate Passover as soon as they crossed into the Promised Land?
4. What lessons was the later Israel to learn from the battle reports of Jericho and Ai and the Gibeon narrative?
5. What do we know about the authorship and date of Joshua?
6. Is Joshua historically accurate?
7. Describe the biblical picture of God as a warrior. Can you think of other places in the Bible not mentioned in this chapter where God is described as acting as a warrior?

chapter eight

THE BOOK
OF JUDGES

Content: What Is Judges About?

The book of Judges narrates events that take place between the death of Joshua (Josh. 24) and the rise of the monarchy (1 Sam. 8–12). For reasons not explained by the biblical text, no single leader inherits the mantle from Joshua, and Israel quickly devolves into a period of moral depravity, spiritual confusion, and political fragmentation. The implied reason for this slide is the lack of a strong, central authority figure who can lead Israel on the path of righteousness (Judg. 17:6; 18:1; 19:1; 21:25).

The book of Judges may be divided into three main parts. The first section (1:1–2:5) describes the continuing conflict with the native inhabitants of Canaan who survived the initial phase of the conquest under Joshua, who is now dead. This section of Judges is often contrasted with the optimistic description of the conquest found in Joshua 1–12.

The most familiar portion of the book of Judges is the large second part (2:6–16:31), which gives the book its name. Here we read of the various judges whom God raises up for Israel. The nature of the office of the judge is not clear across the board. The longest and best-remembered stories concern leaders whom God uses to rid the land of foreign oppressors. These judges sometimes (e.g., Deborah), but not always (e.g., Samson), exercise some administrative leadership as well. Other judges (Tola, Jair, Ibzan, Elon, and Abdon), typically introduced briefly in the book, are not associated with military action, but rather are described as if they are administrators (10:1–5; 12:8–15).

Judges whom God uses to violently remove oppressors from Israel are better understood as "rescuers" rather than judges in the legislative sense (Othniel, Ehud, Shamgar, Deborah, Gideon, Jephthah, Samson). Their stories are often told using formulaic language and in a set pattern (though this may vary at least slightly from judge to judge). The typical pattern begins by noting that "the Israelites did evil in the eyes of the LORD" (3:7, 12; 4:1; 6:1; 10:6; 13:1). While the exact nature of the evil is not usually specified, when it is, idolatry is highlighted (2:11; 7:6). As a consequence of the people's sin, God turns them over to a foreign oppressor (2:14; 3:8, 12; 4:2; 6:1; 10:7; 13:1). But when the people "cried out to the LORD"—a phrase that should be taken as a turn away from their idolatry and back to worship of God (3:9, 15; 4:3; 6:6, 7; 10:10)—God raises up a judge to save them. This part of the story is the most developed section of all and brings each narrative its distinctive style. The work of the judges ushers in a period of peace, but peace only lasts until the next sin of Israel. One gets the feeling of Israel going around in circles or, more accurately, entering into a death spiral, since the judges themselves get increasingly problematic as one moves from the relatively virtuous Othniel, Ehud, and Deborah to the morally compromised Gideon (and his ephod [8:22–27] and son Abimelech [chap. 9]), Jephthah (and the offering of his daughter [11:34–40]), and the laughable, but thoroughly despicable Samson, who does nothing except for his own desires.

The final section of the book departs from the presentation of judges, but the two stories found there have a pattern similar to each other. They give the account of two dysfunctional families, whose problems lead to the description of Israel as a dysfunctional nation. The first story (chaps. 17–18) begins with an Ephraimite named Micah, who confesses to stealing silver from his mother. When he confesses and returns the silver, she takes some of it and praises God by constructing "an image overlaid with silver ... the idol" (17:3, 4). Her spiritual confusion is palpable. She thinks she is praising God, but she is really breaking the second commandment (Exod. 20:4–6; Deut. 5:8–10). Micah sets up a private shrine in his home, and when a Levite wanders by, he hires him to be his personal priest, a travesty of the true worship of Yahweh. Matters get elevated to a national level when some scouts from the tribe of Dan come by in search of a new area for the tribe to settle. The unstated sin is that the tribe is abandoning its God-given land in favor of a place of its own choosing. When the Danites move up to the far north and settle, they steal Micah's idol and persuade the Levite to come with them, anticipating the sin of Jeroboam's false shrine at the city of Dan (1 Kings 12:25–33).

Without going into the same detail, the final story of Judges (chaps. 19–21) also begins with family problems as a Levite's concubine leaves him to return to her father. When he fetches her home, they spend the night in Gibeah in the tribe of Benjamin (Saul's future hometown), which is described in a way that is reminiscent of Sodom and Gomorrah. All the characters in this story are negatively portrayed, and when the men of Gibeah rape and kill the concubine whom the Levite had shoved out the door for them, the Levite rallies the other tribes to wage war on the tribe of Benjamin. The other tribes first impulsively attempt to eradicate the tribe of Benjamin from the face of the earth and then panic when that almost happens, devising all kinds of shrewd ways to keep the tribe alive.

As said before, all the stories of Judges contribute to painting the picture of this era as depraved, confused, and fragmented. "In those days Israel had no king; everyone did as they saw fit" (17:6).

Authorship and Date: Who Wrote Judges and When?

Like so many Old Testament books, Judges is anonymous, and therefore the date of its writing is also not explicitly stated. Thus, whatever we say about authorship and date is speculative and based on hints within the text rather than direct statements.

Reasons exist, though, to think that there was a major edition of the book in the early monarchical period. Indeed, a major purpose of the book seems to be to provide a rationale for or even a defense of the monarchy. In the final chapters there is a refrain that implies that the problems of the period of the judges could be resolved with the institution of a king (17:6). The story of the Levite and the concubine that leads to the war against Benjamin (chaps. 19–21) describes the tribe of Benjamin and Saul's hometown of Gibeah so negatively that some argue for a more precise date during the reign of David, who was still dealing with some who considered David a usurper. If there was a major edition of the book in the early monarchy or even more specifically during David's reign, the book still had not come to its final form, at least if one takes seriously the note in Judges 18:30 that speaks of the exile. While some favor an earlier exile date (of the north, 722 BC), the fact that it is probable that Joshua through Kings reached its final form during the Babylonian exile makes 586–539 BC more likely.

Genre: What Style of Literature Is Judges?

Judges is another example of theological history (see the Excursus on Theological History).

Connections: How Does Judges Anticipate the Gospel?

We have already made much of Judges' anticipation of or support for the rise of the monarchy. Thus we may say that Judges participates in a biblical theology of kingship that has its roots in the Pentateuch's intimations of a future monarchy (Gen. 17:6; 49:9–12; Num. 24:17–19; Deut. 17:14–20). The imperfect leaders known as judges make Israel yearn for something better—a king. However, when God does establish kingship in Israel, it does not remove all moral depravity and spiritual confusion. Indeed, like the judges, most of the kings are themselves imperfect, leading Israel astray. For this reason God chooses to bring human kingship to an end at the time of the Babylonian exile. After kingship disappears, the faithful increasingly realize that the promise of the Davidic covenant that there would be a Davidic king on the throne forever (2 Sam. 7:16) must have a different, deeper meaning. Thus, during the late Old Testament period and into the intertestamental period, there arises an expectation that a Davidic king, a messiah, would come in the future. That Messiah, of course, is Jesus, and that truth is affirmed every time he is referred to as "the Christ" (the Greek equivalent of "Messiah").

Recommended Resources

Block, D. I. *Judges, Ruth.* NAC. Nashville: Broadman & Holman, 2002.

_____. "Judges." Pages 94–241 in ZIBBC 2. Edited by J. H. Walton. Grand Rapids: Zondervan, 2009.

Younger, L. *Judges, Ruth.* NIVAC. Grand Rapids: Zondervan, 2002.

Questions for Review and Discussion

1. The chapter describes the period of the judges as a time of moral depravity, spiritual confusion, and political fragmentation. Give examples.
2. What does the book of Judges say about kingship?

3. What is the pattern used to describe the judges? Read the Jephthah story and identify the pattern in this narrative.
4. When was Judges written? How does its purpose fit in with its date?
5. How does the book of Judges anticipate Christ?

chapter nine

THE BOOK
OF RUTH

Content: What Is Ruth About?

The events of the book of Ruth are set during the time of the judges, a period that the book of Judges characterizes as morally depraved, spiritually confused, and politically fragmented. The story of Ruth, by contrast, presents admirable characters and an uplifting message.

However, the book begins by describing a distressing situation. An Israelite couple, Elimelek and Naomi, leave their hometown, Bethlehem, and travel to Moab to avoid the ravages of a famine. Elimelek dies in Moab, and their two sons marry Moabite women. After a while, the two sons die, leaving behind Naomi and her two Moabite daughters-in-law, Orpah and Ruth. The narrator is not explicitly critical of the Israelite family for leaving Bethlehem, but the question is raised by the fate they met in Moab as well as the fact that other residents of Bethlehem, who apparently did not leave, survived well enough.

Eventually Naomi decides to return to Bethlehem. At first, her daughters-in-law accompany her, though she encourages both of them to stay in Moab since she cannot assure them of husbands in a culture where single women suffer. While Orpah stays in Moab, Ruth is determined to remain with her mother-in-law, declaring, "Where you go I will go, and where you stay I will stay. Your people will be my people and your God my God. Where you die I will die, and there I will be buried. May the LORD deal with me, be it ever so severely, if even death separates you and me" (1:16–17). In this way Ruth gives up her Moabite background and, like Rahab before her (Josh. 2), becomes an Israelite. Naomi ("Pleasant"), though, is not cheered by her situation and changes her name to Mara ("Bitter").

In chapter 2 Ruth goes out to glean in the fields. The law provides for the poor by allowing them to pluck the harvest of others (Deut. 24:19–22). Ruth finds herself in the fields of Boaz, who turns out to be a relative of Naomi's deceased husband, Elimelek. While on the surface her meeting with Boaz seems like a coincidence, the narrator clearly wants the reader to understand that God's providential hand is guiding the action of the story. This story also illustrates the virtue of loyalty. Ruth has been loyal to her mother-in-law, and Boaz is showing loyalty to Ruth and Naomi by providing them with grain.

Naomi encourages Ruth to pursue a marriage relationship with Boaz. He is a near-kinsman, after all, and therefore has certain responsibilities according to custom, presumably seen as an extension of the law of the go'el (or kinsman-redeemer; see Lev. 25:25–30, 47–55; Deut. 25:5–10; cf. Jer. 32:1–15). At Naomi's encouragement, Ruth goes to Boaz as he is sleeping on the threshing floor after harvest and "uncovers his feet" (which some scholars say means having physical contact). Her request that he "spread the corner of your garment over me" (Ruth 3:9) is a request for marriage. While responding that her actions indicate that she is "a woman of noble character" (3:11), Boaz says that he must first deal with a man whose claims are even stronger than his.

In the next scene (4:1–12), Boaz deals deftly with the other claimant, informing him of Ruth's availability in a manner that also reveals that he will incur financial loss if he claims her. The unnamed man declines the offer, and Boaz and Ruth are married. The book ends happily (4:13–22). Boaz and Ruth are married and have a baby. The book concludes with a genealogy demonstrating that this child is an ancestor of the future King David.

The conclusion to the book reflects that a theological-political purpose may have been important for the contemporary audience. That is, it may have indicated that God's providential hand was involved in David's birth and thus implied that providence also brought him to the throne. The book's purpose, however, transcends this narrow political goal. For one thing, the story encourages those who struggle by showing that God can direct events to bring the sufferer to a better place. The core teaching of this book concerns the hidden and continuous providence of God. Another goal is that the book's characters, particularly Ruth and Boaz, provide healthy examples of loyalty (hesed), kindness, and generosity. Indeed, Ruth's placement after Proverbs in the Hebrew Scriptures is not accidental,

since Proverbs ends with a poem about the woman of "noble character" (*'eshet hayil*), an epithet that Boaz attributes to Ruth.

Authorship and Date: Who Wrote Ruth and When?

The book of Ruth is anonymous. We cannot know with certainty
who wrote it or when it was written. That said, the genealogy that
shows King David's descent from Ruth and Boaz likely indicates
that the book was written, perhaps not yet in its final form, during
the reign of David. Some believe that Ruth was written in the postexilic period as a polemic against Ezra and Nehemiah, who forbade
marriage with foreign women (Ezra 10; Neh. 13:23–27). Properly
understood, however, there is no conflict between Ruth and Ezra-
Nehemiah. The latter books worry about intermarriage with pagan
foreign women. Ruth is a woman who gives up her pagan beliefs for
a full acceptance of Yahweh (Ruth 1:16–17).

Genre: What Style of Literature Is Ruth?

Ruth reads like a novella or a short story. While some suggest that the
book is accordingly fictional, we remain unpersuaded that the highly
artistic narration signifies a nonhistorical text. Thus we would identify the book as yet another example of theological history (see the
Excursus on Theological History).

Connections: How Does Ruth Anticipate the Gospel?

Matthew's genealogy of Jesus names only four women, and Ruth is
among them (Matt. 1:5). Ruth was a foreigner, but she is part of the
line that produced the Messiah. The New Testament also provides
the preeminent example of how God's providence leads to redemption. According to Acts 2:23–24, while on a human level Jesus' execution was the result of the plotting and actions of those who hated
him, God's hidden providential hand was behind it, in order to bring
salvation.

Recommended Resources

Block, D. I. *Judges, Ruth*. NAC. Nashville: Broadman & Holman,
2002.

Bush, F. *Ruth, Esther.* WBC. Nashville: Thomas Nelson, 1996.

Hals, R. M. *The Theology of the Book of Ruth.* Minneapolis: Fortress, 1969.

Hubbard, Jr., R. L. *The Book of Ruth.* NICOT. Grand Rapids: Eerdmans, 1988.

Manor, D. W. "Ruth." Pages 242–65 in ZIBBC 2. Edited by J. H. Walton. Grand Rapids: Zondervan, 2009.

Ulrich, D. R. *From Famine to Fullness: The Gospel according to Ruth.* Phillipsburg, NJ: P and R Publishing, 2007.

Younger, L. *Judges, Ruth.* NIVAC. Grand Rapids: Zondervan, 2002.

Questions for Review and Discussion

1. What ancient customs are important to know to understand the plot of Ruth? How do they factor into the story?
2. What role does divine providence play in the book of Ruth? What do we learn about God from the book?
3. How does the story of Ruth connect with King David? with Christ?

chapter ten

THE BOOK OF SAMUEL

Content: What Is Samuel About?

Although presently divided into two parts, the book of Samuel is really a single composition. The major characters of the book are Samuel, the last judge; Saul, the first king; and David, the first of a dynasty of kings. Among these three, none is more prominent than David. The literary quality of the book of Samuel is broadly recognized. The stories are intriguing and compelling.

The book fits neatly into the developing redemptive history begun in Genesis. It picks up the subject of the book of Judges (and Ruth) at the end of the period of judges (eleventh century BC) and narrates the rise of the monarchy (into the early tenth century BC). The book of Kings will continue the story, beginning at the precise point where Samuel ends. First Chronicles 10 – 29 provides a synoptic account of the end of Saul's reign and the entirety of David's. The relationship among these books will be further discussed under authorship in the chapter on Kings.

The book of Samuel opens with a focus on Samuel (chaps. 1 – 7), the last judge and the one who helps usher in the institution of kingship. His birth to the barren Hannah by the intercession of God indicates his future importance. Indeed, his mother's celebratory song (2:1 – 11) anticipates the rise of kingship (v. 10). Hannah dedicates her long-hoped-for son as a Nazirite (Num. 6:1 – 21) and turns him over to Eli, the judge, to serve in the tabernacle. The narrative draws a subtle contrast between Samuel and Eli and the latter's sons. While Samuel follows the Lord, Eli's sons are wicked (2:12 – 26). While

Samuel is sensitive to God's voice, the physically flabby Eli is also spiritually flabby and cannot discern God's voice (chap. 3).

Under Eli's judgeship and his sons' leadership of the army, conditions worsen. The Philistines are able to defeat the Israelite army and capture the ark of the covenant, which Eli's sons were treating as no more than a magical box (4:1–11). When Eli hears the news, he falls off a chair, breaks his neck, and dies (4:12–22). The ark meanwhile is taken away to Ashdod and placed in the temple of Dagon as a prize of war. The Lord, however, makes the Philistines aware that he is able to exert his power over them by causing the statue of Dagon to crash onto the floor twice. God also causes disease to break out in Philistia until the ark is returned to Israel. This first section of Samuel closes with an account of Samuel leading Israel as they defeat the Philistines at Mizpah (7:2–17).

In the next major section (chaps. 8–12) we witness the introduction of kingship to Israel. While kingship is anticipated earlier, in the Pentateuch (Gen. 17:16; 49:8–12; Num. 24:17–19; Deut. 17:14–20), its rise is not initiated by God, but by the elders of the people who ask for a king out of fear rather than confidence in God. Even so, God chooses to use this moment to introduce the first king, but that process is fraught with tension, and the choice of the first king is less than ideal. God tells Samuel to anoint the young Saul as first king, and he does so when Saul and a comrade come to the prophet to get help to find lost donkeys. After anointing him, Samuel tells Saul that certain events will befall him, indicating that God is behind his anointing. These events include having the Spirit of the Lord come on him at Gibeah, where, Samuel emphasizes, there is a Philistine garrison. After the Spirit comes on him, Saul is to "do whatever your hand finds to do, for God is with you" (10:7). Though vaguely stated, it is clear that the Spirit is to give him (as the Spirit gave the judges) the ability to defeat the garrison. Once this is done, Saul is to meet Samuel at Gilgal (see 10:1–8). In spite of these instructions, however, and despite the fact that all the anticipated signs occur, Saul does not defeat the Philistine garrison or go to Gilgal. Instead, he returns home, where he keeps his anointing a secret (10:9–16), a signal that he is unwilling to step up to the task God has for him.

Samuel next makes Saul's kingship public at Mizpah. Even when the lots choose him as king, Saul is found hiding among the baggage (10:23). Yet the people are impressed with their reluctant king because he is taller than anyone else. Finally, Saul follows through on his kingship by rallying to deliver the city of Jabesh from the Ammonites (chap. 11). Thus Saul is confirmed as king (11:12–15). The section ends with a covenant renewal ceremony. The people, who had threatened their relationship with God because of their request for a king, reaffirm their willingness to follow the Divine King (chap. 12).

Saul's introduction as king is therefore filled with foreboding, and the next few chapters (13–15) show clearly that he is not a leader who can please either God or his people. Due to his lack of confidence in God as his warrior (since the number of troops he has would not determine the outcome; Deut. 20:8), Saul forfeits the possibility of a dynasty (1 Sam. 13:13–14). And due to his unwillingness to carry out the command of God to eradicate the Amalekites (chap. 15; cf. Exod. 17:15; Deut. 25:17–19), he forfeits his own rule.

Thus God turns his attention away from Saul and to David, who is anointed by Samuel. Saul was made king because he was tall; David is chosen because of his heart (16:7). Even so, David does not assume the kingship immediately, because Saul is still alive. Indeed, David enters his service as a musician to soothe Saul's tormented soul (16:14–22), anticipating his place as the composer of many of the psalms. He is also introduced as a warrior when he takes on Goliath in the power of God (chap. 17).

Soon Saul grows jealous and suspicious of David, driving him from the court. The narrative depicts Saul as paranoid and unfair to David. And David, although he is anointed as the next king, is not interested in assassination (chaps. 24 and 26). He awaits God's timing and tries to keep distance from Saul. Even so, while in exile, David is accompanied by the high priest Abiathar and a prophet named Gad as well as an army of six hundred. David is the leader of a nation in exile. Nonetheless, the narrator emphasizes the fact that David does not manipulate, but waits on God. At the end of the first book of Samuel, Saul ends his life, by suicide, as pitiably as he lived it (chap. 31).

The opening of 2 Samuel emphasizes David's sadness at the death of Saul and Saul's son Jonathan (chap. 1), who was one of David's best friends. David is immediately proclaimed king of Judah, but the north makes Ish-Bosheth, a son of Saul, their king. Ish-Bosheth's champion is Abner, the head of Saul's army, while Joab is the head of David's military. War breaks out between the north and the south. After being slighted by Ish-Bosheth, Abner offers to turn the north over to David. Joab reacts angrily to David's agreement with Abner, who had earlier killed the commander's brother Asahel. Without David's knowledge, Joab meets up with Abner and assassinates him. The narrative shows David expressing anger over Joab's act and sadness over Abner's death (3:22–39). Next, two northern leaders assassinate Ish-Bosheth, but when they report this to David, he executes them. The narrative is careful in its attempt to exonerate David from either of these political assassinations, but these actions open up the north to him, and he is soon proclaimed king in the north (5:1–5).

The next few chapters record important victories and accomplishments. David conquers Jerusalem and establishes it as the capital of his kingdom, beholden to no individual tribe (5:6–16). He also defeats the Philistines (5:17–23), and soon thereafter the narrator speaks of "rest from all his enemies around him" (7:1; note also the summary of David's victories in 8:1–14). This rest triggers in David a desire to build God a permanent dwelling on earth: a temple to replace the tabernacle. After all, Deuteronomy 12, the law of centralization, notes that once God gave Israel rest from its internal enemies, he would choose a place that would become the only place where sacrificial worship could take place. However, God rejects David's initiative, because it is up to God to choose the place and the time. David will not build a "house" for God, but God will build a "house" for David: a dynasty of kings. Second Samuel 7 thus establishes a "covenant" of kingship between God and David (v. 28). (This covenant is reaffirmed in Psalms 89 and 132.) As opposed to Saul, David is a king after God's heart (1 Sam. 13:14), and his descendants will follow him on the throne.

David's kingdom continues its rise until his encounter with Bathsheba (chap. 11). The narrator subtly criticizes David for not being on the battlefield (11:1) and falling into sin when he spies the bathing Bathsheba, whom he lures into his bed. To make matters worse, David attempts to cover up his sin by calling her husband, Uriah, back from the battlefield so that he will sleep with her and thus think the baby is his. However, Uriah refuses, perhaps because he realizes that having sex will render him ritually unclean (Lev. 15:16–18) and unable to return to the battlefield, where God's special presence is indicated by the ark. Uriah, who is a Hittite, observes the little details of the law, while David, the king, breaks major commandments. Since Uriah will not sleep with his wife, David takes the even more drastic step of having him killed on the battlefield. But David does not succeed in keeping his sin a secret, because he is confronted by Nathan the prophet. David repents and restores his relationship with God (chap. 12), but his sin still has horrible consequences. First, the child dies. Then David's family falls apart. His son Amnon rapes his half-sister Tamar and is then killed by her brother Absalom (chap. 13). Absalom is then banished for a period of time, but is eventually permitted to return. He foments rebellion against his father and succeeds in deposing him for a while, although David eventually restores his kingship (chaps. 15 – 19). Other rebellions (chap. 20) and internal turmoil (chap. 21) follow.

The second book of Samuel ends with an appendix that breaks the narrative flow of the book. This section contains a hymn and the "last words of David" (22:1 – 23:7) as well as a list of David's mighty men (23:8 – 39). The final chapter records the time when David sins by taking a census of the fighting men, likely exposing a lack of confidence in God and overconfidence in his fighting forces. God punishes David with a three-day plague, and David buys the threshing floor where God's death angel stopped the plague. He builds an altar there, an anticipation of the temple that will eventually be constructed at this location (chap. 24).

Authorship and Date: Who Wrote Samuel and When?

Samuel is anonymous. Early Jewish tradition names Samuel as the composer of 1 Samuel 1 – 24, and the rest is attributed to the prophets Nathan and Gad (*Baba Batra* 14b), but this is unlikely. There are many theories about the compositional history of the books of Samuel but they are all highly speculative and not helpful for understanding the book. The fact that at least parts of the book appear to be an apology for David's presence on the throne probably indicates that some form of the book existed at the time of David. However, it is likely that the book achieved its present shape during the exile at the same time as the book of Kings, with which it now forms a seamless whole.

Genre: What Style of Literature Is Samuel?

The book is written in prose narrative for the most part, but the poems occupy a special place in the final composition. Hannah's prayer in 1 Samuel 2:1 – 10 and David's songs in the appendix (2 Sam. 22:1 – 23:7) create a frame around the book as a whole, raising the main theme of the whole book—kingship. Hannah's prayer anticipates the rise of kingship, while the concluding poems speak to how a king should live before God.

The prose narrative portions present theological history (for which see the Excursus on Theological History) from the eve of the period of the Judges to the eve of David's reign. They chronicle the rise of kingship as an institution in Israel with particular attention to the importance of the Davidic dynasty. Indeed, as noted above, the book has indications of being a royal apology for David and his dynasty. The story line highlights how David comes to the throne, distancing him from the charge of pushing Saul and his heirs out and promoting the idea that his reign is the result of divine election. (See in particular the Davidic covenant of kingship in 2 Samuel 7.)

Connections: How Does Samuel Anticipate the Gospel?

The single most important connection of the book is found in the Davidic covenant (2 Samuel 7). Here we find the promise to David that "your house and your kingdom will endure forever before me; your throne will be established forever" (v. 16). As history progresses, it becomes clear that with few exceptions (Hezekiah and Josiah, most notably) David's sons will not follow him in his devotion to God. They lead Israel astray and into exile. The monarchy itself comes to a close with the removal of Zedekiah (597 – 586 BC) and the Babylonian destruction of Jerusalem. Since that time, no human descendant of David has ruled.

During the late Old Testament period and into the period between the Testaments, it became increasingly clear that God's promise was deeper than previously imagined and his people hoped for someone better to lead them, a descendant of David who would be an anointed king (messiah). The New Testament understands that person to be Jesus the Christ, the Messiah, the son of David who rules forever (Rom. 1:1 – 6).

Recommended Resources

Boda, M. J. *After God's Own Heart: The Gospel according to David.* Phillipsburg, NJ: P and R Publishing, 2007.

Borgman, P. *David, Saul, and God.* Oxford: Oxford University Press, 2008.

Gordon, V. P. *1 and 2 Samuel*. Grand Rapids: Zondervan, 1988.

Long, V. P. "1 Samuel." Pages 266 – 411 in ZIBBC 2. Edited by J. H. Walton. Grand Rapids: Zondervan, 2009.

_____. "2 Samuel." Pages 412 – 91 in ZIBBC 2. Edited by J. H. Walton. Grand Rapids: Zondervan, 2009.

Provan, I., V. P. Long, and T. Longman. *A Biblical History of Israel*. Louisville, KY: Westminster John Knox, 2003.

Questions for Review and Discussion

1. First Samuel 1 – 7 describes the end of the period of judges. How do these chapters compare with the picture given of the same time period in the book of Judges? In the book of Ruth?
2. Is kingship a divinely authorized institution? How should the human king relate to God, the Divine King?
3. Compare Saul and David as people. As kings.
4. What are the consequences of David's sin with Bathsheba?
5. What is the purpose of the book of Samuel in the light of its connection with Kings and the time of its final composition?
6. How is the Davidic covenant fulfilled in the New Testament? In 2 Samuel 7?

chapter eleven

THE BOOK OF KINGS

Content: What Is Kings About?

Kings continues the history of Israel begun in Samuel. The book of Kings opens by describing the twilight of David's reign and ends with an account of the destruction of Jerusalem and even a short note of the release of King Jehoiachin from Babylonian prison (2 Kings 25:27–30). The time period therefore is from the beginning of the tenth century to the middle of the sixth century BC, though of course the narrative is highly selective.

When the book begins, Adonijah is making a bid on the throne of his father, supported by powerful elements within the country (Joab the general and Abiathar the priest). Bathsheba and Nathan intercede with the aged David, who responds by making Solomon king, charging him to remain obedient to God and giving him instructions on how to consolidate his kingdom (1 Kings 1:1–2:12).

Solomon's reign is the focus of 1 Kings 2:13–11:43. His reign begins well. After consolidating his power, he demonstrates a devout spirit by asking God for wisdom. God is so pleased with this request that he also grants Solomon riches and honor (3:13). The following chapters illustrate how Solomon governs with a wisdom that achieves an international reputation. At the center of his early achievements is the construction of the temple, for which his father prepared. David completed the subjugation of Israel's internal enemies, making it appropriate for his son, whose very name means "Peace," to construct the building that represents Israel's establishment in the land. Unfortunately, Solomon's reign does not end as it began. He married many foreign women, and they turned his heart away from the true God. He also oppressed the northern tribes.

Accordingly, the northern tribes rebel against the Davidic dynasty once Solomon is dead (1 Kings 12–14). The northern tribes refuse to recognize Solomon's son Rehoboam as king and instead anoint Jeroboam, a former Solomonic official who had rebelled against his master and sought political refuge in Egypt. Jeroboam then constructs two shrines for the worship of golden calves in the south (Bethel) and in the north (Dan) of his country, even though God warned him against it through an unnamed prophet (chap. 13).

The bulk of the narrative is then devoted to a history of the two kingdoms in which the writer shuttles back and forth between the accounts of the overlapping reigns of the kings in each kingdom (1 Kings 15–2 Kings 17). The account of the reign of a king in one kingdom is followed each time by an account of the reign of the king or kings in the other kingdom who came to the throne during his reign. For example, the account of Asa's reign in the southern kingdom (Judah; 1 Kings 15:9–24) is followed by accounts of Nadab, Baasha, Elah, Zimri, Omri, and Ahab (15:25–16:34), all of whom came to the throne in the northern kingdom (Israel) during Asa's reign. The reign of Jehoshaphat (1 Kings 22:41–50), the king who followed Asa in the South, is taken up only after the report of Ahab's death. The narrative fluctuates between reigns in the North and South until the northern kingdom is carried into exile by the Assyrians. Judah remains alone as the spiritual successor of the kingdoms (2 Kings 18–25), and her history is reported until the Babylonian conquest, the destruction of Jerusalem, and Jehoiachin's release from prison during captivity.

Genre: What Style of Literature Is Kings?

Kings continues the genre of theological history begun in Genesis. The book intends to recount the past (witness the frequent citation of court records; for instance, "the annals of the kings of Judah" [e.g., 1 Kings 14:29; 15:7; 2 Kings 8:23; 12:19; 14:18; 24:5], "the annals of the kings of Israel" [e.g., 1 Kings 14:19; 15:31; 2 Kings 1:18; 10:34; 13:8, 12], and "the book of the annals of Solomon" [1 Kings 11:41]). But like all history writing, the book does so very selectively and for a purpose. That purpose, as we will see below, is evident as compared with the book of Chronicles, since the two cover the same period of time but with different emphases.

Purpose, Authorship, and Date: Who Wrote Kings, When, and Why?

The purpose of Kings is closely bound with the question of when Kings was written, so in this section we will treat these topics together. As mentioned above, the purpose of Kings comes into clear outline when compared with Chronicles. As a general rule, while Chronicles gives a positive portrayal of the history of Israel, Kings is negative. An example may be seen in the respective books' portrayal of the reign of King Abijah. In 2 Chronicles 13, Abijah is presented as a good and godly king; in 1 Kings 15:1–8, he is thoroughly bad. In matters of detail, Kings names the negative Absalom as his "father," while Chronicles substitutes the nonentity Uriel of Gibeah. In addition, the Hebrew text refers to Abijah ("my father is Yahweh") as Abijam ("my father is Yam," an obvious reference to the sea, a symbol of chaos) in order to further darken his portrait. While these two portraits of Abijah may be harmonized, what is of most interest is Kings' intentional negative portrayal not only of this king but of the history of Israel. Why do the authors of Kings paint the history of Israel in a negative light? That will be the focus of this section; for the comparable question concerning Chronicles, see that chapter.

The answer to the question of the book's purpose for its portrayal of Israel's history is found in the date when it was written, or better stated—since it is likely that the book as we know it existed in two or three editions before it became fixed—when it came into its final form. The date of the composition of the final form of the book can be determined by observing the last event that the history records. Second Kings 25:27–30 describes the release of King Jehoiachin from Babylonian prison during Evil-Merodach's reign. Jehoiachin had been taken into captivity by Nebuchadnezzar in 597 BC (2 Kings 24:8–17). The Babylonian captivity began in earnest in 586 BC. Evil-Merodach's reign was short-lived, 562–560 BC. The latter, then, is the date when the book was written. The fact that the book's composition happened in the midst of the exile is clear also from the absence of mention of the Persians' defeat of Babylon and the Cyrus Decree in 539 BC.

Noting the exilic date of the composition of the final form of the book, we can discern the purpose of writing such a negative rendition of the history of Israel. The book intends to answer the question, "Why are we in exile?"

The answer is found in Israel's rebellion against God. Kings then rehearses the history of Israel and examines how well its people have kept the law of God, particularly as the law is expressed in the book of Deuteronomy. The authors, who are anonymous, examine the kings and people of Israel as to whether they kept the law of centralization, the law of kingship, and the law of the prophets.

The law of centralization (Deut. 12) insists that Israel — once God gives them rest from all their enemies (12:10) — should bring their sacrifices only to the place that God chooses. The place God chooses is a reference to the temple in Jerusalem, so each king is evaluated as to whether or not he preserves the exclusive worship of the Lord in the temple. The results are telling. In the North, rather than worshiping God in the temple, Jeroboam for political reasons builds two shrines in Dan and Bethel and tells his people to worship there. Every king thereafter is judged as to whether or not he perpetuates Jeroboam's sin, and all of them do. In the southern kingdom, the kings are judged based on keeping the temple free from idols and on allowing worship in the so-called "high places," shrines built up on the hills. Again, the results are not good. While some kings (such as Jehoshaphat; 1 Kings 22:43 – 44) keep the temple pure, they allow for the high places. Only two kings (Hezekiah and Josiah) keep the law of centralization with full integrity. Thus Kings answers the question, "Why are we in exile?" by noting the infraction of the law of centralization.

Second, Deuteronomy 17:14 – 20 describes God's will concerning the character and actions of Israel's future kings. The king should be pious, devoted to the law. He should avoid riches, large harems, and large armies. When we read the history of Israel in the book of Kings with this text in the background, we have the second answer to the question as to why Israel was in exile. Their kings did not live up to God's standard as delineated in the law of kingship in Deuteronomy.

The third Deuteronomic law that is relevant to the book of Kings concerns the prophet (Deut. 13:1 – 5; 18:14 – 22). This law (in two parts) gives Israel principles by which they can tell the true from the false prophet. True prophets speak in God's name; false prophets do not. A true prophet's signs come true, not so a false prophet's. The history in Kings describes how God sends true prophets, but they are rejected by the kings and the people, while the false prophets with their happy news are readily embraced (see 1 Kings 13 for a particularly interesting example).

Because Israel breaks the Deuteronomic law, according to Kings, the curses of the covenant come into effect. The Deuteronomic curses describe judgments such as those that came on Israel, including siege, defeat, and exile (Deut. 27–28).

Finally, we should mention that Kings puts an emphasis on delayed retribution. When a king sins, the punishment for that sin may be delayed for a considerable period of time. For example, Jeroboam's sin in building the golden calf shrines in Bethel and Dan is not fully punished for centuries. While he builds the shrines in the tenth century BC, it is not until the time of Josiah (640–609 BC) that the prophetic announcement of doom is realized (see 1 Kings 13:1–3 and 2 Kings 23:9–18). Delayed retribution is yet another way that the author of Kings explains the exile. The Israelites are suffering in exile not only because of their personal sins, but for the accumulated sins of the centuries before.

In conclusion, the date of the final composition of Kings is during the Babylonian exile sometime after 562–560 BC, the time given for the release of Jehoiachin from Babylonian prison. The purpose is to explain to God's people why they were suffering in exile. The purpose is served by surveying Israel's history through the lens of the Deuteronomic law. For this reason, although the author (or authors) is unknown, he (or they) is often referred to as the Deuteronomic historian.

Connections: How Does Kings Anticipate the Gospel?

The book of Kings has many themes that connect to the New Testament, but none so significant as that of kingship itself. In the chapter on Judges, we saw how the imperfections of the judges led to a hope for something better, namely kingship. The book of Kings (and Samuel before it) describes the failure of kingship in general to provide the leadership that would allow Israel to maintain a deep and rich relationship with God. Indeed, the book makes it clear that the kings are a large part of the problem as they worship other gods and sin against their subjects. The end of the book of Kings narrates the monarchy's demise and the exile. It almost seems as if the story of Israel and its kings is over. Kings ends, however, with a glimmer of hope as it tells of King Jehoiachin's release from Babylonian prison (2 Kings 25:27–30). Even during exile and under foreign domination, divine favor still attends David's descendants. The New Testament shows that this same hope was alive in Israel during the days of Roman rule. The gospel writers are concerned to trace the Davidic ancestry of Jesus and his rightful claim to the title "son of David," heir to the kingdom that God would erect as a consequence of his promises to David (Matt. 1:1, 6, 17, 20; 9:27; 12:23; 15:22; 20:31; 21:9, 15; Mark 10:47–48; 11:10; Luke 1:27, 32, 69; 2:4; 3:31; 18:39; John 7:42).

Recommended Resources

Brueggemann, W. *1 and 2 Kings*. SHBC. Macon, GA: Smyth and Helwys, 2000.

Dillard, R. B. *Faith in the Face of Apostasy: The Gospel according to Elijah and Elisha*. Phillipsburg, NJ: P and R Publishing, 1999.

Konkel, A. H. *1 and 2 Kings*. NIVAC. Grand Rapids: Zondervan, 2006.

Monson, J. "1 Kings." Pages 2–109 in ZIBBC 3. Edited by J. H. Walton. Grand Rapids: Zondervan, 2009.

Provan, I. *1 and 2 Kings*. NIBCOT. Peabody, MA: Hendrickson, 1995.

_____. "2 Kings." Pages 110–219 in ZIBBC 3. Edited by J. H. Walton. Grand Rapids: Zondervan, 2009.

Questions for Review and Discussion

1. What is the nature of the differences between Kings and Chronicles?
2. What contemporary issues is the author of the book of Kings addressing?
3. What strategy does the author of the book of Kings use to answer the questions raised by the situation at the time the book was completed?
4. What is the law of centralization, and how does it help shape the book of Kings?

chapter twelve

THE BOOK
OF CHRONICLES

Content: What Is Chronicles About?

The book of Chronicles begins with genealogies that start with Adam, so in a sense it provides a history of humanity stretching from the beginning up to its present, the postexilic period. Of course, this account is extremely selective, particularly from Adam through Saul. The main focus is on the period from David to the issuing of the Cyrus Decree. Thus the bulk of the book covers the same historical period as the latter part of Samuel through 2 Kings. A review of these two histories presents quite a contrast. While Kings selects negative stories about Israel's past, Chronicles largely narrates positive ones. The reasons for these different historical presentations will be discussed below under Purpose.

The book begins with an extensive section on genealogies (1 Chron. 1–9). These genealogies serve to show the postexilic generation's connection to the past, going all the way back to Adam. All the tribes, even the northern tribes that have been in exile for almost two centuries, are included with a genealogy (with the exception of Zebulon and Dan). Even though only Judah (and some Levites) was exiled to Babylon and is returning to Jerusalem, the inclusion of northern tribes shows that God's people have not lost a sense of "all Israel," an important theme in the book (1 Chron. 9:1; 11:1, 10; 12:38; 14:8; 15:3, 28; 18:14; 2 Chron. 1:2; 7:8; 9:30; 10:3, 16; 12:1; 13:4, 15; 18:16; 24:5). This concern may be the result of not only a wistful look at the past, but also a hope for the future. The genealogies may also have served a very practical function in the postexilic period, answering questions such as who is able to be priest (Neh.

7:61–65). Issues of social status, military obligation, land distribution, and hereditary rights are also in part addressed by these genealogies. Modern readers may find these chapters tedious, but they serve an important practical and theological purpose in the book.

The second major part of Chronicles follows the United Monarchy (1 Chron. 10—2 Chron. 9). While the history in Samuel devotes many chapters to the rise of the monarchy (1 Sam. 8–12) and Saul's turbulent rule (1 Sam. 13–31), Chronicles narrates only his death, which it attributes to the fact that he was "unfaithful to the LORD" (1 Chron. 10:13). The transition to David is reported as a smooth one in that "all Israel" comes together in Hebron to affirm him as their new king (11:1). Samuel chooses to give more detail, describing how it took seven and a half difficult years after David was proclaimed king of Judah for him to be declared king of Israel (2 Sam. 5:1–5). The omission of the negative complications of the transition is typical of the overall presentation of the reigns of David and Solomon. The story of David's sin with Bathsheba and its consequences in the Absalom rebellion and the account of the turmoil at the time of the transition from David to Solomon are not found in Chronicles. Solomon's marriage to foreign women and the resultant apostasy are not given as the reason for the schism between the North and the South. Rather, Rehoboam's demands and Jeroboam's rebellion are the causes (2 Chron. 10).

However, not all the negative stories are absent from Chronicles. David's sin concerning the census that had such horrible consequences is retained (1 Chron. 21; cf. 2 Sam. 24). The differences here and elsewhere between Chronicles and Samuel-Kings are not an attempt at a cover-up of Israel's tawdry past, but as we will see below, Chronicles' positive history (as well as the exceptions, as in 1 Chron. 21) is explained by the needs of the contemporary audience of the book.

A second difference in the telling of the story of the United Monarchy may be seen in Chronicles' heavy emphasis on the building of the first temple. David is concerned to move the ark back to Jerusalem early in his reign (1 Chron. 13–16). He may not build the temple, but he expends tremendous resources to prepare for his son to do so (1 Chron. 22–27). When power is transferred from David to Solomon, there is an emphasis on the future building of the temple (1 Chron. 28–29). Then, of course, substantial narrative is devoted to the actual building of it (2 Chron. 2–7). The reasons for this emphasis will be given below.

The last part of Chronicles records the events of the Divided Monarchy all the way to the exile (2 Chron. 10–36). It even goes a bit further than the account in Kings in that it also reports the so-called Cyrus Decree that the Persian king issues after he defeats Babylon (2 Chron. 36:22–23). The Cyrus Decree permits the Jews to return to Jerusalem from their captivity in Babylon.

A number of differences between Kings and Chronicles in the presentation of the Divided Monarchy are explained by the different purposes of these two historical works (see Purpose below). In the first place, the emphasis here is solidly on Judah rather than the northern kingdom. Indeed, the northern kingdom is only included if it is relevant to the history of the South. After all, it is only Judah that is returning from the exile; thus the northern kingdom is not immediately relevant to the Jewish people who constituted Chronicles' original audience. This emphasis explains, for instance, why the long chapters in Kings concerning the prophets Elijah and Elisha—who combated the Baal worship of the northern king Ahab and his queen, Jezebel—are not included in Chronicles.

In the second place, as with the account of the United Monarchy, there is less emphasis on the negative events of this period. For instance, a look at the reign of Abijah shows that the Kings account is thoroughly negative (1 Kings 15:1–8), while the one in Chronicles is thoroughly positive (2 Chron. 13). Even in the case where it was impossible to ignore the negative influence of a king's reign, we can detect differences. According to Kings and Chronicles, there was no king worse than Manasseh (see 2 Kings 21:1–18; 2 Chron. 33). That said, Chronicles informs us of something that Kings chooses not to report. At the end of his life, Manasseh repents and restores his relationship with God (2 Chron. 33:10–20). Chronicles probably chooses to include an account of his repentance not only to present a more positive portrait of the king, but also because of the book's interest in promoting a doctrine of immediate retribution. The writer wants to explain why such a wicked king had such a long reign and died in old age. While the Deuteronomic historian in Samuel-Kings emphasizes delayed retribution to explain the exile, Chronicles includes stories of immediate retribution. Such a concern may explain the shape of Chronicles' description of Josiah's death. How could such a good king die facing a pagan king like Pharaoh Neco? Chronicles explains that God warned Josiah not to prevent Neco's army from proceeding north. One might sympathize with Josiah, considering that God chose to use Neco himself as the one who delivers the divine message, but Chronicles makes it very clear that God was speaking through Neco and that Josiah ignored the divine command (1 Chron. 35:20 – 36:1). The reason for this emphasis on immediate retribution will be given below.

Genre: What Style of Literature Is Chronicles?

Chronicles continues the genre of theological history begun in Genesis and, like all historical writing, does so selectively and for a purpose (see the Excursus on Theological History). The purpose, as we will see below, is evident as compared with the book of Kings, since the two cover the same period of time but with different emphases. Like Kings, Chronicles also cites sources (see 1 Chron. 27:4; 29:29; 2 Chron. 16:11; 24:27, for example).

Purpose, Authorship, and Date: Who Wrote Chronicles, When, and Why?

As with Kings, the purpose of Chronicles is closely bound with the question as to when the book was written, so in this chapter we will treat these topics together. As mentioned above, the purpose of Chronicles comes into clear outline when compared with Kings. As a general rule, while Chronicles gives a positive portrayal of the history of Israel, Kings is negative. The reason for this difference is found in that Chronicles is set at the time the book reached its final form. Because the final event narrated in the book is the Cyrus Decree, allowing the Jewish people to return to Jerusalem after the Babylonian exile (2 Chron. 36:22 – 23), it is clear that the book was written for people in the period of the restoration or postexilic period rather than, like Kings, during the exilic period.

People had vastly different questions in mind after the exile. No longer was it necessary to explain the reasons for the exile. The new questions included "What is our connection with the past?" and "How do we act now?" These questions explain the emphases of the book of Chronicles as described above under Content. There we saw that Chronicles starts with nine chapters of genealogy. What better way to show connection to the past? The postexilic generation could see that it was related to those people before the incredible disruption of the destruction of Jerusalem. They were connected to previous glorious days like the time of David and Solomon. They were related to the patriarchs Abraham, Isaac, and Jacob, who had received the promises (Gen. 12:1–3). They even went back all the way to Adam.

The interest in Judah to the diminishment of the role of the northern kingdom can also be explained by the time of the original writing. Only Judah returned from exile. Thus it was Judah's story that mattered.

Further, the intense interest in the building of the first temple can be explained by the fact that the postexilic community constructed the second temple. It is likely that Chronicles was written (though perhaps not fixed in final form) in the early postexilic period before or during the time that the temple was being built under the leadership of Sheshbazzar and Zerubbabel (520–515 BC). The excitement and preparation for the building of the first temple would inspire them as they constructed the second. We should also note that the reason why Chronicles includes the account of David's sin concerning the census is that, in spite of the fact that it usually does not select negative stories about David, the story ends with the purchase of the threshing floor of Araunah (1 Chron. 21:25), the future location of the temple.

Finally, the reason for the emphasis on immediate retribution is obvious as well. The anonymous authors of Chronicles were not interested in giving reasons for the exile, but rather in preventing future problems. An emphasis on immediate retribution would help discourage sin that would lead to divine judgment. It is much more likely that the people will obey if they realize that God will punish them in the present rather than a distant descendant in the future.

In summary, Chronicles was written by an unknown author (or authors) sometime in the postexilic period (post–539 BC). While many indications point to the early postexilic period, some material seems to be added later. (For instance, Zerubbabel's genealogy in 1 Chronicles 3:19–24 seems to continue until after the time period of Ezra-Nehemiah and thus into the late 400s.) We can refer to the author as the Chronicler. His purpose was to answer the questions that his contemporaries were asking: "What is our connection with the past? What do we do now?"

Connections: How Does Chronicles Anticipate the Gospel?

Chronicles, like all the books of theological history, narrates how God works for the restoration of his people. This divine work is deeply embedded in the covenant promises that were given to Abraham (Gen. 12:1–3). This redemptive history tells the story that will ultimately climax in Jesus Christ, who fulfills the Old Testament covenant. Chronicles, like Kings, also tells the story of the various kings who ruled in Israel and Judah. Those who descended from David and who rule in Jerusalem do so on the basis of God's covenant of kingship with David (2 Sam. 7; 1 Chron. 17). The book of Kings emphasizes the ultimate failure of these kings in a way that points to something better—the true anointed King, Jesus. Chronicles, however, gives the reader a much more positive assessment of the kings. In particular, Chronicles describes David and Solomon in their full messianic splendor in a way that anticipates the glory of David's greater Son.

Recommended Resources

Dillard, R. B. *2 Chronicles*. WBC. Nashville: Thomas Nelson, 1987.

Mabie, F. J., and S. Sherwin. "1 Chronicles." Pages 220–85 in ZIBBC 3. Edited by J. H. Walton. Grand Rapids: Zondervan, 2009.

Mabie, F. J. "2 Chronicles." Pages 286–393 in ZIBBC 3. Edited by J. H. Walton. Grand Rapids: Zondervan, 2009.

Williamson, H. G. M. *1 and 2 Chronicles*. NCB. London: Marshall, Morgan, and Scott, 1982.

Questions for Review and Discussion

1. In what ways does the history in the book of Chronicles differ from that in Kings?
2. How does the date of the composition of the book of Chronicles affect the shape of its presentation of history?
3. Why does the book of Chronicles devote so much attention to the construction of the temple?
4. What purpose do the genealogies in 1 Chronicles 1–9 serve?
5. Why does the book of Chronicles emphasize immediate retribution?

chapter thirteen

THE BOOK
OF EZRA-NEHEMIAH

Content: What Is Ezra-Nehemiah About?

While Ezra and Nehemiah are counted as two books in our Bibles, they originally were one and will be treated as one in this chapter. Historically speaking, the book has two major parts: Ezra 1–6 is written in third-person narration and concerns the early postexilic period from the time of the Cyrus Decree (539 BC) to the time of the completion of the second temple (515 BC). There is a brief section that concerns a later period, when Xerxes (485–465 BC) and Artaxerxes I (465–424 BC) ruled (4:9–24). The second major part is written mostly in the first person (by Ezra and Nehemiah) and concerns the period between 458 and 433 BC.

The book opens with Cyrus's decree that the Jewish people be allowed to return to Jerusalem to rebuild the temple. Cyrus, the great Persian king, has just defeated Babylon and inherited its vast empire, including the province of Judah. He attempts to win the favor of the vassals—including the Jewish people, previously exiled by the Babylonians—by allowing them to return. As the Cyrus Cylinder reveals, this act is not out of favoritism toward the Jews, but rather a part of a broader Persian policy. Still, from a Jewish perspective, it is a fulfillment of prophetic expectation. The initial leaders of the return are Sheshbazzar and Zerubbabel, the latter a Davidic descendant. As soon as they return, they rebuild the altar and begin to offer sacrifices there for the first time since the Babylonian destruction of Jerusalem (Ezra 3:1–6). They then rebuild the foundation of the temple (3:7–13), but work falters as opposition arises from their enemies, described as those who had been imported by the Assyrians into the area (probably the region of the former northern kingdom). The mention of this opposition leads the narrator to speak of later opposition at the time of Xerxes and Artaxerxes (4:9–24) before returning to the main subject.

In response to the work stoppage, God raises up two prophets, Haggai and Zechariah (Ezra 5:1)—whose oracles are found among the Minor Prophets—to stir the Jewish people back to the task of rebuilding the temple. In spite of further opposition, Darius, who by this time had become king of Persia (and reigns 522–486 BC), permits the building to go on, and the temple is finished in 515 BC.

The second major part of the book (Ezra 7–Nehemiah 13) begins with a description of Ezra's return to Jerusalem. Ezra was a scribe and a priest, a descendant of Aaron (7:3–6). After a short third-person introduction to Ezra, the narrative switches to a memoir written by Ezra himself (Ezra 7–10 and Nehemiah 8–10). Ezra's return is said to be in the seventh year of Artaxerxes' reign. Most scholars today believe this refers to Artaxerxes I, and thus Ezra's arrival in Jerusalem would be in 458 BC.

Ezra is specifically commissioned by the Persian ruler to restore the law in Jerusalem. Again, this Persian policy is not the result of any favoritism toward the Jewish people, but the way the Persian emperors attempt to keep order in the provincial areas of their vast empire. When he returns, Ezra has to attend in particular to the sin of intermarriage (chaps. 8–10). Jewish men have been divorcing their Jewish wives and marrying pagan women, a sin that led to Israel's troubles in the first place.

Nehemiah is introduced for the first time in Nehemiah 1, where he is serving as cupbearer to Artaxerxes, an extremely important position in the royal court. Nehemiah's brother informs him about the sad state of the city of Jerusalem. The king notes his depression and agrees to send him back to Jerusalem as the governor of the province of Judah in 445 BC. Again, this move is in keeping with broader Persian policy that encouraged the development of cooperative vassal states in the empire as a bulwark against Persia's mortal enemy Greece. In any case, though he returns with the blessing of the emperor, Nehemiah runs into local opposition to his restoration of Jerusalem—particularly its walls—but through his courage and determination and faith, he successfully restores the city's walls (Neh. 6:15–7:3).

The book concludes with a renewal of the covenant now that the law has been reinstituted and the wall and the city have been restored. The people affirm their commitment to God (9:38–10:39).

However, the book does not end on a positive note. The final chapter (13) records Nehemiah's complaints about the continuing sin of the people and his attempts to stop it. In other words, the book does not end with a triumphal note of restored and continuing harmony between the Jewish people and their God or among themselves, but with the account of continuing problems.

Authorship and Date: Who Wrote Ezra-Nehemiah and When?

While early Jewish tradition names Ezra the author of Ezra-Nehemiah, the book is anonymous. The book contains two memoirs, Ezra's (Ezra 7–10 and Neh. 8–10) and Nehemiah's (Neh. 1–7 and 11–13), written in the first person, but they are included in a third-person narration (particularly Ezra 1–6). Therefore the final author is not known, though it is not impossible that it was Ezra. The earliest date of writing would be after the last events that are narrated, so the book was finished sometime after 433 BC. At one point it was thought that Ezra-Nehemiah was part of the Chronicler's historical project (see the chapter on Chronicles), but this view is not widely held today.

Genre: What Style of Literature Is Ezra-Nehemiah?

Overall, Ezra-Nehemiah is theological history (see the Excursus on Theological History), but it includes letters, royal edicts, and lists. The book is unique among the theological historical books of the Old Testament by including memoirs by Ezra and Nehemiah. A memoir is a first-person writing that is distinguished from autobiography by the fact that the former concentrates on events observed by the writer while the latter focuses on the self who is doing the writing. The use of the memoir form gives the writing a more personal and subjective viewpoint.

Connections: How Does Ezra-Nehemiah Anticipate the Gospel?

As noted above, Ezra-Nehemiah does not end on a note of resolution. Problems remain among the people of God. While the events recorded in this book show an initial fulfillment of the prophetic oracles of salvation, one is left with the feeling of more that is to come. That more is the subject of the Gospel.

In addition, Ezra-Nehemiah speaks of an age of separation. God wanted his people to stay separate from the Gentiles. The law served as a spiritual wall of separation, as in particular the ritual law created a strong demarcation between Jew and Gentile. Ezra and Nehemiah's passionate protest against mixed marriages also speaks to this need to be separate. The physical wall that Nehemiah's men constructed was yet a different type of separation. It was Jesus Christ who would tear down this "wall of separation." First of all, he tore apart the veil that separated the Holy of Holies from the rest of creation. Second, he demolished the division of humanity that separated Jew from Gentile (Eph. 2:14–18).

Recommended Resources

Green, D. "Ezra–Nehemiah." Pages 206–15 in *A Complete Literary Guide to the Bible*. Edited by L. Ryken and T. Longman. Grand Rapids: Zondervan, 1993.

McConville, J. G. *Ezra, Nehemiah and Esther*. DSB. Louisville, KY: Westminster Press, 1985.

Yamauchi, E. M. *Persia and the Bible*. Grand Rapids: Baker, 1990.

_____. "Ezra and Nehemiah." Pages 394–467 in ZIBBC 3. Edited by J. H. Walton. Grand Rapids: Zondervan, 2009.

Questions for Review and Discussion

1. What is the genre of Ezra-Nehemiah? Is there anything unique about its constituent parts?
2. Compare and contrast the leadership styles, roles, and achievements of Ezra and Nehemiah.
3. Who is Zerubbabel? When did he live, and what did he accomplish?
4. How did God use the Persians in his plans for Judah during this time period?
5. How does the book end, and what is the significance of this ending?

chapter fourteen

THE BOOK OF ESTHER

Content: What Is Esther About?

While Ezra-Nehemiah provides a window into postexilic life in Judah, Esther is set in the Diaspora, among those Jewish people who chose not to return. Set during the reign of the Persian king Ahasuerus (most translations use his Greek name, Xerxes [485–465 BC]), the story, as we will see, deals with ancient animosities.

The story begins with a great banquet thrown by King Xerxes. Indeed, much of the action of the book is set in banquets, culminating in a feast, Purim, that will become an annual tradition among the Jewish people. The purpose of the king's banquet is to display his wealth, power, and authority. Perhaps this feast is the same as that mentioned by the Greek historian Herodotus, which preceded a campaign against the Greeks. The king's authority, however, is put into question by the refusal of Queen Vashti to present herself before the crowds. Xerxes thus deposes her and eventually searches for a new queen.

It is in this context that we meet the main characters of the book, Mordecai and Esther, who are cousins. Mordecai is identified as a Benjaminite and descendant of Shimei and Kish (2:5), a fact of great significance for the story. We also learn that Esther is beautiful, so when the king seeks his new wife by sleeping with a number of women, we are not surprised—though early rabbinic interpreters are disturbed by this—that Esther is found to be more attractive than the others, and she is taken as his queen. At the same time, we learn that Mordecai, who must be closely related to the court, foils an assassination plot against the king (2:19–23).

In chapter 3 we meet the last major character of the book, Haman, son of Hammedatha, the Agagite. The king promotes him to a high position, but Mordecai refuses to pay respect to him, and Haman in turn hates not only Mordecai, but all the Jewish people.

Thus Haman persuades the king to issue an edict that will allow the enemies of the Jewish people to eradicate them. They throw the *purim* (or "lots") to determine a date, about a year in the future.

Mordecai, however, catches wind of the plot and seeks Esther's help. She at first refuses, until she is reminded that she too will meet a horrible fate (chap. 4). She approaches the king and requests that he and Haman join her for a banquet (5:1–8).

Before that banquet, the action shifts back to Haman, who expresses his hatred for Mordecai and his people to his wife and friends (5:9–14). They advise him to do away with Mordecai, and he builds a seventy-five-foot sharpened stake on which to impale him. Haman is now truly happy as he contemplates joining the king and his queen for dinner and also ridding himself of his enemy.

Unfortunately for Haman, however, the king has a sleepless night and asks to hear stories out of his royal chronicles (6:1). The fact that they just so happen to read about Mordecai's exposure of the assassination plot may seem like a coincidence, but the attentive reader knows that here (as throughout) we see the providence of God. When Haman arrives the next morning thinking that he is the one whom the king wants to honor, he recommends that the king grant the recipient of his gratitude his royal cloak and horse and that he be led through the streets of Susa by a trusted advisor. The first of many ironic reversals of this story takes place when the king tells Haman to do this for the hated Mordecai.

The second major ironic reversal takes place at Esther's banquet when she reveals to the king Haman's plot against the Jewish people (chap. 7). The king responds by ordering Haman to be impaled on the sharpened pole he had prepared for Mordecai.

Nonetheless, the king is not above his own law, so he cannot rescind his permission for the Jewish people's enemies to attack them on the appointed day. However, he can and does issue a second decree that allows the Jewish people to arm themselves and attack their enemies (chap. 8).

The conclusion of the story describes the great victory of the Jewish people over their enemies (9:1–17). These are not just any enemies either. The fact that Mordecai is a Benjaminite related to Shimei and Kish connects him with King Saul. The fact that Haman is an Agagite connects him to the Amalekites. Specifically, it reminds the attentive reader that Saul had the opportunity and the responsibility to eradicate the Amalekites under the command of King Agag (1 Sam. 15). After all, God had issued a decree for the complete annihilation of the Amalekites stemming back to Exodus 17:1–7 (see also Deut. 25:17–19). Saul did not follow through on his responsibility, but a later descendant follows through on what he neglected to do.

Authorship and Date: Who Wrote Esther and When?

The book of Esther is anonymous, and the date of writing is not clear, though it clearly follows sometime after the events recorded, which take place during the reign of Ahasuerus (Xerxes; 485–465 BC).

The book accounts for the origins of Purim, an annual festival still observed by Jewish people today. It celebrates the Jews' victory over their long-standing enemies, who tried to destroy them.

Genre: What Style of Literature Is Esther?

Like Ruth, Esther has been cataloged as a short story or novella, often with the implication that it is a work of fiction. However, the highly artistic nature of the storytelling does not preclude the idea that the book is telling a story that, at least in its broad outline, actually happened in space and time. Debate will continue, since, while classical and cuneiform sources by and large demonstrate the author's familiarity with Persian mores and court life, there remain some problems with the historical details of the book.

Connections: How Does Esther Anticipate the Gospel?

Esther tells the story of the survival of the Jewish people in the face of almost certain (at least from a human perspective) extinction. If they had been annihilated, it would have meant the end to the fulfillment of the covenant promises, including that of a Messiah. Here in a distant city hundreds of miles and several centuries removed from events in Judah, God still providentially ruled the course of history and brought it steadily to the appearance of his own Son, who would break down the barrier between Jew and Gentile (Gal. 3:28).

Recommended Resources

Bush, R. W. *Ruth, Esther*. WBC. Dallas: Word, 1996.

Jobes, K. *Esther*. NIVAC. Grand Rapids: Zondervan, 1999.

Tomasino, A. "Esther." Pages 468–505 in ZIBBC 3. Edited by J. H. Walton. Grand Rapids: Zondervan, 2009.

Questions for Review and Discussion

1. What is the significance of Mordecai's relationship to Saul and Haman's to Agag?
2. What role do banquets play in the plot of Esther?
3. Name the ironic reversals in the book of Esther.
4. Who is the hero of the book of Esther? Why do you think so?
5. What role does God play in the book?

EXCURSUS ON
THEOLOGICAL HISTORY

Theological history describes the genre of much of the Old Testament from Genesis through Esther. "Remembrance" is important to biblical religion (Deut. 7:18), since God acts in history to save his people and to judge those who oppress them. While not all narrative texts are necessarily historical (e.g., Job) and not all historical texts are concerned with the same measure of precision of historical reporting (e.g., Gen. 1–11), historical narrative is important in the Old Testament.

When reading historical narrative in the Old Testament, it is important to make a distinction between writing about past events and the events themselves. Historical narrative is a representation of the events and involves literary artifice. It is right to regard Old Testament narrative as storylike histories. V. P. Long, for instance, has made an analogy between history writing and portrait painting. A portrait is not the person, but a representation of that person. One can do different portraits of the same person and, while not capturing the whole person, can give a reliable reflection of that person or at least one aspect of their personality. Provan, Long, and Longman have written a history of Israel with the awareness of the representational nature of Hebrew history writing.

History writing is selective, emphasized, and interpretive. Historians cannot write about every event that is relevant to their topic and must be selective, choosing those events that are "important." What is important emerges from the intention of the writer. For example, in the chapter on Kings, we explain that the author is concerned to answer the question, "What did Israel do to deserve the exile?" This intention shapes the selection and interpretation as well as the emphasis that the history gives to the events of Israel between the time of Solomon and the exile.

Some histories are written with a focus on economics, warfare, or politics. While the Bible speaks to these areas of Israel's life, it does so only as they interact with its main purpose, which is to tell about God and his relationship with his people. For this reason, we call biblical history "theological history."

This general description of theological history in the Bible is supplemented by issues that are specific to individual biblical books in the various chapters of this book.

Recommended Resources

Long, V. P. *The Art of Biblical History.* Grand Rapids: Zondervan, 1994.

Longman, T. "History and History Writing." In *Hearing the Old Testament.* Edited by C. Bartholomew and D. Beldman. Grand Rapids: Eerdmans, forthcoming.

Provan, I., V. P. Long, and T. Longman III. *A Biblical History of Israel.* Louisville, KY: Westminster John Knox, 2003.

chapter fifteen

THE BOOK
OF JOB

Content: What Is Job About?

The book of Job tells the story of a man, Job, from the city of Uz (outside the land of Israel). The prose prologue (chaps. 1–2) describes Job as "blameless and upright" and a person who fears God (1:1, 8; 2:3). He also enjoys great rewards from the hand of God. At the urging of the Accuser (which is what "Satan" means), God puts Job to the test. Will he reject (curse) God if God does not reward him for his piety? At first the Accuser removes his wealth and his children, but Job remains faithful to God (1:13–22). The Accuser receives permission from God to intensify the test by assaulting Job himself with a horrible but unspecified disease, yet he still maintains his relationship with God (2:7–10). At the end of the prose prologue, Job's three friends—Eliphaz, Bildad, and Zophar—come and comfort him by sitting with him in silence.

At this point the composer turns from prose to poetry as Job breaks the silence by uttering a complaint (chap. 3). He never curses God, but neither does he follow the example of the psalms of lament by speaking to God and asking him to change his circumstance. Instead, he asks why he was ever born.

In what is the longest section of the book (chaps. 4–27), the three friends and Job engage in an increasingly intense debate over the cause of his suffering. Eliphaz, Bildad, and Zophar all argue that Job suffers because he is a sinner. They have a harsh and mechanical understanding of retribution theology. If you sin, then you suffer. Therefore, if you suffer, it is because you are a sinner (Eliphaz:

4:7–11; 5:2–7; 15:20–35; Bildad: 8:3–4, 11–21; 18:5–21; Zophar: 11:11; 20:5–29). Job's only hope is to repent and then God will restore him (5:8–16, 23–27; 8:5–7; 11:13–20; 22:22–30). Job is correct to argue that he is not suffering because he is a sinner, a point made very clear in the prose prologue. However, Job operates with the same retribution theology as his three friends. Thus he believes God is unjust to let him suffer (9:22–24). While at first he expresses doubt that it will help (9:3, 19–20), he grows in his determination to speak to God and set him straight (in the dialogues themselves, but climactically in 31:35–37).

While Job and his friends debate why Job is suffering and how he can escape his pain, the real issue is who is wise. Wisdom includes the ability to diagnose a problem and prescribe a solution. The three friends and Job all set themselves up as a source of wisdom and belittle the wisdom of the other party (8:2; 11:2–3, 12; 12:2–3; 16:2–3).

The debate reaches an impasse when the three friends realize that they cannot convince Job to repent. They grow silent, but Job continues to speak. In chapter 28 he delivers an exquisite poetic monologue that describes God, not humans, as the source of all wisdom. This anticipates the conclusion of the book, but in the very next chapter Job falls right back into complaint as he remembers his previous blessed condition (chap. 29) to contrast it to his present misery (chap. 30). After protesting his innocence one more time (chap. 31), he falls silent, hoping to get an audience with God in order to charge him with injustice.

Job will get his audience, but before that happens, a hitherto unannounced new character appears—Elihu—who proceeds to berate the three friends for failing to convince Job and also berates Job for not repenting (chaps. 32–37). While representing his position as something new, Elihu falls back on the same old retribution theology of the three friends. What is different is what he claims to be the source of his wisdom (remembering that the book is ultimately a debate about the source of wisdom). He claims that his wisdom comes from the spirit of God (32:8) and not from the experience of advanced age (like the three friends). However, the fact that no one bothers to answer him shows that his wisdom, like all human wisdom, falls far short.

The book achieves resolution at the end with the appearance of God and Job's repentance (38:1–42:6). God never tells Job why he suffered, but instead describes his great wisdom and power. When Job repents (first in 40:3–5 and then in 42:1–6), he does not repent of sin that led to his suffering in the first place (there was no such sin), but rather of his falsely accusing God of injustice (see 40:8).

The book ends with a prose epilogue (42:7–17). First God speaks to Eliphaz, who represents the three friends and tells them that they must ask Job to offer an intercessory prayer and sacrifices on their behalf because they have misrepresented God as one who works in a rigid way with sinners and the righteous. Then God restores Job's wealth and gives him a new family.

The main purpose of the book is to show that God is the only source of true wisdom, thus exposing the inadequacy of all human wisdom. Suffering is the issue that leads to the debate over wisdom. While the book is not about suffering, the story also makes the point that suffering is often mysterious in its origin. Much of the Bible does suggest a link between sin and suffering. The law, for instance, teaches that obedience leads to reward and disobedience to punishment (Deut. 27–28). The book of Kings gives an account of the history of God's people in order to make the case that they deserved the exile because of this sin. God sends the prophets in order to challenge the people to repent of their sins or face horrible consequences. Proverbs instructs its readers that the wise and godly way leads to life, while the ungodly, foolish way leads to death. By describing the main character as a righteous, God-fearing man who suffers horribly, the book of Job makes it clear that not all suffering is related to sin.

Authorship and Date: Who Wrote Job and When?

Some, but not all, ancient tradition attributes the writing of the book of Job to Moses (*Baba Batra* 14a). The reasoning seems to be that the action of the book of Job is early (pre-Abrahamic), and therefore the writing must be early—an argument that does not follow. Job is thus one of a number of anonymous writings in the Old Testament, whose date of writing is also unclear and, moreover, unimportant to the interpretation of the book.

Scholarship presents many reasons to think that Job was not written at a single sitting, but developed over a long period of time. There are many variations on this theory, but a common one begins with the belief that the prose prologue (chaps. 1–2) and the prose epilogue

(42:7–17) preexisted the poetical parts. The debate between Job and the three friends (chaps. 3–27, maybe including 29–31) was then added in order to provide a discussion of the reasons for Job's suffering. God's response and Job's repentance may have been added at this time as well. It is often thought that Elihu's speeches and the poem concerning wisdom (chap. 28) were among the last parts of the book of Job to be added.

Such a view of the development of the book of Job is possible, but speculative. The power and truth of the book do not depend on whether it was written by one person at one time or many people over a period of time. In either case, the modern interpreter should make the final form of the book the object of study, since that is canonical for believing communities today.

Interestingly, the plot of the book of Job takes place outside of the Promised Land, since Uz is most likely located in the region later known as Edom in present-day Jordan. However, the setting of the action of the book tells us nothing about where the book was written. Most likely the book was written in Israel, although as we have already indicated, we do not know precisely *when* the book was written.

Genre: What Style of Literature Is Job?

In many ways Job is like no other literature, and some scholars describe the book as defining its own genre. On the other hand, many have suggested particular genre labels, including dramatized lament, "forensic" literature, tragedy, comedy, drama, parody, and apocalyptic literature.

While there are elements of most of the genres listed, the main issue of the book concerns wisdom. Wisdom involves the skill of living, the ability to navigate life's pitfalls and difficulties. The book describes Job's suffering as a problem needing a solution. Each of the human characters presents his understanding of the reason why Job is suffering as well as a prescription for a solution. The three friends promote their own ideas while ridiculing Job's, and vice versa. Elihu chimes in as well. Thus the genre of the book may best be identified as a "wisdom debate." None of the human characters of the book wins this debate. At the end, the book reveals God as the only true source of wisdom when he speaks to Job out of the whirlwind. Job grows silent and submits to God's overwhelming power and wisdom (42:1–6), thus demonstrating the "fear of the LORD" that defines true biblical wisdom (Prov. 1:7).

Connections: How Does Job Anticipate the Gospel?

As explained above, the main message of Job is that God is the source of all wisdom. Not surprisingly, then, the New Testament presents Jesus as the apex of God's wisdom. The Gospels describe how Jesus in his youth grew in wisdom and demonstrated it in front of the temple officials (Luke 2:40 – 52). He later taught in parables, the teaching vehicle of the sage, and astounded his hearers with the depth of his wisdom (Mark 1:27). Paul proclaimed that "in him [Christ] are hidden all the treasures of wisdom and knowledge" (Col. 2:3). As God himself, Jesus manifested the wisdom of God. He is the source of all true wisdom.

Jesus connects to Job in yet another way. Job and Jesus are the only two people in the Bible who are presented as truly innocent sufferers. But here the similarity ends. While Job suffered against his will, Jesus suffered voluntarily. Job's pain teaches those who read about it a lesson about life, but Jesus' suffering is on behalf of sinners to bear their punishment and save them.

Through the history of interpretation, many have been tempted to treat Job's desire for an umpire ("mediator," 9:33) or "redeemer" (19:23 – 29) as a veiled prophecy of Jesus. It is more likely that Job is thinking of an angel who would take up his case in heaven. That said, in large measure Job's desire for an advocate in heaven is surpassed in the reality of Jesus far beyond what Job could have imagined.

Recommended Resources

Jackson, D. R. *Crying Out for Vindication: The Gospel according to Job.* Phillipsburg, NJ: P and R Publishing, 2007.

Longman, T. *Job.* BCOTWP. Grand Rapids: Baker, 2012.

Seow, L. *Job.* Grand Rapids: Eerdmans, forthcoming.

Zerafa, P. P. *The Wisdom of God in the Book of Job.* Rome: Herder, 1978.

Questions for Review and Discussion

1. What viewpoint does Job adopt about his suffering? How about the three friends? How about Elihu? How about God?
2. With which character of the book should we associate its message?

3. What is the main theme of the book? What contribution does the book make to that theme?
4. What do we learn about suffering in the book of Job?
5. What is retribution theology, and how does the book of Job contribute to the biblical view on it?
6. Compare and contrast Job and Jesus.

chapter sixteen

THE BOOK OF PSALMS

Content: What Is Psalms About?

The book of Psalms is a collection of 150 songs that served as the hymnbook of the Old Testament people of God. The songs are in poetic form and are largely addressed to God, so may also be called prayers. The songs were collected over almost a thousand years (from the time of Moses [mid-second millennium BC] to the late postexilic period [perhaps as late as 300 BC]). The largest number of psalms is attributed to David (who ruled 1004–965 BC).

The final form of the Psalms is divided into five books (Pss. 1–41; 42–72; 73–89; 90–106; 107–150), reflecting the fivefold division of the Torah (Genesis, Exodus, Leviticus, Numbers, Deuteronomy). The editors who so divided the psalms likely intended to thus assert that the Psalms, though human prayers to God, have the same divine authority as the Torah. The psalms are God's word to his people.

In spite of efforts to find an overarching editorial structure to the book of Psalms, no clear-cut structure has been found that has convinced readers. The book is not organized chronologically, thematically, generically, or in any other discernable manner.

That said, it does appear that Psalms 1 and 2 were intentionally placed at the beginning of the book as an introduction, signaled by the fact that neither has a title. Psalm 1 describes the blessing that will come on the righteous and the difficulties that will confront the wicked. This psalm serves as a kind of gatekeeper to the book of Psalms, comparable to the role played by the priestly gatekeepers at the sanctuary. The sanctuary was a holy place, and only the righteous could enter — those who meditate and keep the law of God; the gatekeepers would keep the wicked and ritually unclean outside. In the same way, the readers of Psalm 1 would identify themselves as either righteous or wicked with the implicit understanding that the wicked should proceed no further. After all, the Psalms are a holy textual place, a literary sanctuary. The psalms are prayers spoken in the presence of God. One must be righteous to enter the holy place, whether physical or textual (see Pss. 15; 24:3–6). Once readers enter the sanctuary of the Psalms, they encounter God and his Messiah (Ps. 2). While the messiah, or anointed one, was the Davidic king who ruled from Jerusalem during the monarchic period, the Messiah took on eschatological significance during the postexilic period, when the psalms received their final structure and order. Thus, in the final form the Messiah was that future king who would come in fulfillment of the Davidic promise that there would be a king who ruled forever (1 Sam. 7:11b–16). Therefore the opening of the Psalms introduces the reader to two major themes that reverberate throughout the book as a whole: Law and Messiah.

Furthermore, the final five psalms (146–50) also appear to be intentionally placed at the end in order to serve as a conclusion to the book as a whole. The Hebrew phrase *hallelu Yah* ("praise the LORD") occurs throughout these poems, and the praise reaches a crescendo in Psalm 150. Thus these five psalms serve as a doxology, singing praises to God as the reader exits the "literary sanctuary."

While there does not appear to be a clear-cut reason for the placement of the other psalms in their present order, it is significant to note that the beginning of the book has a predominance of laments that give way to a predominance of hymns toward the end. If this observation is accurate, then the movement of the psalms from lament to hymn reflects how God can turn "wailing into dancing" in the words of Psalm 30:11.

Authorship and Date: Who Wrote the Psalms and When?

As mentioned in the previous section, the book of Psalms is composed of 150 songs collected over a thousand-year period. Thus no one individual wrote the book, but the titles of individual psalms associate them with particular people or groups. The titles are superscripts that precede the psalm itself and, besides naming people or groups, will on occasion give other information, such as the type of psalm (*maskil, miktam, shiggaion,* song, psalm), the occasion of writing, tune, ritual purpose, and more. The status of the titles is debated among scholars. They are not given verse numbers in English translations, though they are in the Hebrew originals, and there is no persuasive reason to doubt that a title preserves helpful and reliable information about the psalm that follows it.

A good example of a title is the one that precedes the well-known penitential psalm, 51: "For the director of music. A psalm of David. When the prophet Nathan came to him after David had committed adultery with Bathsheba." This title connects the psalm with the event recorded in 2 Samuel 11 – 12 and fits that occasion perfectly. The title then states that David wrote this psalm when Nathan confronted him about sleeping with Bathsheba.

If one takes the titles seriously, they name the following contributors to the book of Psalms: Moses, David, Solomon, the sons of Korah, Asaph (a priestly musician), and Ethan the Ezrahite. However, a number of psalms do not have titles or have titles that do not name the composer and are therefore anonymous.

Accordingly, the book of Psalms was a growing collection of songs written by a number of different people over a long period of time. Indeed, although some psalms are anonymous, their content dates them to the period of the exile (586 – 539 BC; see Ps. 137) or even later (Ps. 126).

At some point an anonymous editor placed the book of Psalms in its final order. Of course, this editor worked after the final psalm was written, so it was sometime in the postexilic period.

Genre: What Style of Literature Is Psalms?

Poetry

The book is an anthology or collection of poems. They are specifically lyric poems, the expression of the inward feelings of the composer. As Hebrew poetry, the individual psalms are composed of brief poetic lines that often separate into stanzas. The terseness of the poetic line results in compact meaning, so the reader must slow down and reflect on the poem and resist the temptation to skim over the surface. Brevity is achieved by the spare use of conjunctions and direct object markers. The second colon (that is, rhythmical unit) of the poetic line also elides elements of the first colon, so that the second is often shorter than the first.

The terse poetic line is frequently marked by parallelism, where the second — and in a number of cases, the third or more — colon furthers or sharpens the thought of the first colon. We may see this sharpening in the parallel line in Psalm 6:1:

> LORD, do not rebuke me in your anger
> or discipline me in your wrath.

In the first colon, the psalmist requests that God not verbally assault him, while in the second he carries this thought further by asking God not to take a negative action toward him. We might also note intensification in the prepositional phrase where the Hebrew word for "anger" is replaced by a word that expresses even more passion: "wrath."

While some handbooks on Hebrew poetry go on to describe a number of different categories or types of parallelism, the best analysis simply asks, how does the second (and third or more) colon intensify, sharpen, or further the thought of the first colon? A final example comes from Psalm 1:1:

> Blessed is the one
> > who does not walk in step with the wicked
> or stand in the way that sinners take
> > or sit in the company of mockers. . . .

This verse is a three-part parallelism. The opening "Blessed is the one who" is elided from the next two parts, but the thought carries forward to them. All three parts distance the blessed person from association with sinners. The intensification is seen in part in the words for bad people. Wicked people are bad, but not as much as sinners, and the worst of all are mockers. The last not only are evil, but make fun of the innocent. There is also intensification in the degree of association with bad people. To walk with someone is to be aligned with them, but not as closely as to stand with them. The most settled association is represented by sitting down with someone.

Brevity and parallelism are joined by a heightened use of imagery as the third major characteristic of Hebrew poetry. Much biblical imagery is created by comparison, some explicit (simile) and some implicit (metaphor). Imagery informs a reader about something hard to understand by comparing it to something in everyday experience. Much of the Psalms' description of God is figurative. God is a shepherd (Ps. 23), a warrior (Ps. 98), a king (Ps. 96), a mother (Ps. 131), and the list goes on and on. Unpacking a metaphor involves reflecting on how x is like y. How, for instance, is God like a shepherd? He is not like a shepherd in every way. As one considers the comparison in the light of the content of Psalm 23, the reader learns that God guides, cares for, and protects his sheep (the people of Israel). Reading Psalm 23 in the light of the rest of the Bible and the use of the shepherd image elsewhere in the ancient Near East leads to the conclusion that it is also a royal metaphor. In the ancient Near East, kings were shepherds of their people.

Some of the imagery of the Psalms is derived from ancient Near Eastern mythological texts. One well-known example is the frequent representation of God as the one who defeats, controls, and dominates the waters and its monsters. Ancient Canaanite and Mesopotamian myths describe how their gods so treat deities who represent the waters. The Babylonian Enuma Elish, for instance, describes how the god Ea defeats Apsu, the god of the waters, and then builds his throne on top of his carcass, in a way that sounds familiar to Psalm 29:10, where God builds his throne on the floodwaters. Baal's defeat of the many-headed sea monster Lotan is reflected in the language describing God's defeat of the many-headed Leviathan (the Hebrew equivalent of the Ugaritic name). There are many examples of the use of ancient Near Eastern myths in the Psalms that show that Yahweh, Israel's God, is the only God, so actions and attributes given to other gods are only rightly applied to him.

While brevity, parallelism, and imagery are the leading characteristics of Hebrew poetry as used in the Psalms, there is also a host of secondary poetical devices that were at the disposal of the composers of the psalms. Various sound and word plays can be observed in the Hebrew original, though these are difficult and often impossible to reproduce in English translation. One interesting and recognizable secondary poetical device used in the Psalms and elsewhere in the poetry of the Bible is the acrostic. In an acrostic, the poet would begin each successive unit of poetry with a word that begins with a successive letter of the Hebrew alphabet. Psalm 119 is the best-known example, since English translations typically show how the verses of each eight-verse stanza begin with a successive letter of the Hebrew alphabet.

Songs

The psalms are poems and need to be carefully and slowly read, since poetry carries substantial meaning in just a few words. These poems were meant to be sung, so we may also call them songs.

There are a number of indications that psalms were sung. A large number of psalms have a title that identifies the poem as a song (Heb. *sir*; 30, 45, 46, 48, and more). A Hebrew word often translated "psalm" (*mizmor*; the English word *psalm* comes from the Greek equivalent *psalmos*) also occurs numerous times and comes from a verb that means "make music" or "sing praises" (3, 4, 5, 6, and more). Psalm 18 has a more extended introduction that says, "Of David the servant of the LORD. He sang to the LORD the words of this song...." The titles also include what are universally understood to be the names of tunes (for instance, the title of Psalm 22 says, "To the tune of 'The Doe of the Morning'").

The body of the psalm will also frequently refer to singing. Psalms 96 and 98 both begin with "Sing to the LORD a new song...." Psalm 28:7 proclaims, "With my song I praise him."

While there is little question about the musical nature of the book of Psalms, we do not know much for certain about the music of ancient Israel. Particular instruments are mentioned (ram's horn, tambourine, lyre), but we do not know tunes or melodies. Nonetheless, it is correct to think of the book of Psalms as the hymnbook of the people of God during the Old Testament period.

Types of Psalms

While the psalms as a group may be called poems or songs, they may also be divided into different types, three major and four minor. The major types of psalms are hymn, lament, and thanksgiving. The minor types are remembrance, confidence, wisdom, and kingship.

Hymns

Hymns are songs for moments of joy when life is going well. The singer of a hymn rejoices in his relationship with God and with others. Hymns may be recognized almost immediately by their tone of celebration. Often a reason for praise is given.

Psalm 98 is a good example, beginning with a call to "Sing to the LORD a new song ..." (98:1). The first stanza (vv. 1–3) calls on Israel to praise God for rescuing them in the past. The second stanza

(vv. 4–6) calls on all the inhabitants of the earth to praise God for his being King in the present. The third stanza (vv. 7–9) calls on all creation, including inanimate creation, to praise God for being the Judge who will come in the future.

Laments

Laments are songs for the hard times of life. They have a tone of anger, disappointment, fear, doubt, or shame. They express difficulties in relationship with others (often called the "enemy") or with God, and often in a sense of personal failure. Interestingly, however, most lament psalms turn to God in joy at the end or at the least express a glimmer of hope for rescue from the bad situation in which the psalmist finds himself.

Psalm 69 is a lament in which the psalmist invokes God to come and help him in his trouble (vv. 1a, 13–18). Laments are often brutally honest, and this psalm is no exception, with three separate complaints addressed to God (vv. 1–4, 7–12, 19–21). While some psalms contain a protest of innocence (Ps. 26), this psalm also includes a confession of sin (69:5–6) and also an imprecation, or curse, against those who are persecuting him (vv. 22–28). In spite of all this, the psalm concludes with a hymn of praise (vv. 30–36).

Thanksgiving

When God hears and responds to a lament and rescues the psalmist from trouble, the psalmist responds with a thanksgiving song. It has a joyous tone similar to the hymn, but the thanksgiving remembers the previous lament.

Psalm 30 begins like a hymn exalting God, but quickly cites God's rescue as the reason for joy ("I will exalt you, LORD, for you lifted me out of the depths," v. 1). In verses 6–12 the psalmist remembers how troubled his life was during a period when God abandoned him due to his presumption. He turned from God, and God turned from him. When the psalmist felt the loss of God in his life, he prayed to God to return and God restored him, turning his "wailing into dancing" (v. 11).

Remembrance

Many psalms look to the past to see God's hand in history. A handful of psalms make this the main focus of celebration. They rehearse

God's mighty acts in the past in order to evoke praise from God's people and inspire them with confidence and hope. Psalm 136 is a particularly interesting example in that it is also clearly a liturgical poem in which each verse ends with "His love endures forever." The worship leader — likely a priest — would speak the first half line, and the congregation would respond with the refrain. After general praise of God, Psalm 136 then speaks of creation and then celebrates the exodus from Egypt and the military victories in the wilderness, anticipating the conquest of the land.

Confidence

Psalms of confidence are easily recognized by their tone of quiet trust in God. They are typically brief and have a striking metaphor that supports the emotional quality of the song. Psalm 23 is the classic example, reflecting on God as the Shepherd of his people. Such psalms served to calm the anxieties of the people by reminding them that God is in control.

Wisdom

Biblical wisdom is the practical skill of living, but it is also deeply theological, since its foundation is the "fear of the LORD" (Ps. 111:10; also Job 28:28; Prov. 1:7; 9:10; 31:30). The wisdom literature of the Old Testament (Job, Proverbs, Ecclesiastes) utilizes certain themes and phrases and deals with certain issues (see the chapter on Proverbs), some of which are found in the Psalms. Since proverbial wisdom imparts guidance for living, it has a close connection to the law, so poems that are concerned with the law (Ps. 119) are considered wisdom psalms.

Psalm 1 is a good example. It opens with a blessing (a form familiar from wisdom) on those who avoid evil. It makes a sharp distinction between the righteous and the wicked, categories related to wisdom and folly in the book of Proverbs. The righteous are said to meditate on the law of God.

Kingship

Kingship, too, is a theme that permeates the Psalter. Indeed, if the titles that ascribe authorship of almost half of the psalms to David are taken seriously, then the first-person speaker is none other than the king himself.

But kingship psalms are those psalms whose content speaks of a king, either the human king (Pss. 20, 21) or the Divine King (Pss. 93, 96). Psalm 47 is an excellent example of the latter type; here God is proclaimed King by his people as he mounts his throne to their great praise.

Connections: How Does the Book of Psalms Anticipate the Gospel?

The book of Psalms is the second-most-quoted Old Testament book in the New Testament (after Isaiah). The authors of the New Testament obviously saw the Psalms as anticipating the coming of Jesus Christ. Indeed, Jesus himself spoke to his disciples about how he fulfilled what was written about him in "the Law of Moses, the Prophets and the Psalms" (Luke 24:44). Granted, "Psalms" here stands for the entire third section of the Hebrew canon (the Writings), but certainly includes the book by that name, which stands at the head of this collection.

But what is the connection between the book of Psalms and Jesus? How are Christians to read the psalms as pointing to Christ?

In the first place, the psalms are prayers and songs addressed to God in worship. The New Testament understands Jesus to be God himself; the early church used the language of the second person of the Trinity. Thus these prayers are rightly spoken to Jesus. In the second place, the New Testament speaks about Jesus as the greater "son of David" (Matt. 22:41–46). So he is the Messiah, the anointed King. Jesus in the New Testament is not only the recipient of the worship of the psalms, but also one who sings praises in the assembly with his "brothers and sisters."

We might suggest three ways of reading a psalm to see how it anticipates Christ.

First, we observed earlier how the psalms describe God through the use of relationship metaphors. God is, to give two examples, a shepherd and a warrior. As we turn to the New Testament, we note that Jesus is called the "good shepherd" (John 10) and a warrior who defeats Satan on the cross and battles for us even now against the spiritual powers and authorities (Eph. 4:7–8; Col. 2:13–15). The Christian reader of these psalms naturally thinks of Jesus Christ.

Second, the psalms may be read as prayers *to* Jesus. For instance, Psalm 131 expresses utter confidence in God. The Christian has even more reason to be confident in God thanks to the finished work of Christ (Rom. 8:31 – 39).

Third, the psalms may be read as prayers *of* Jesus. Think of Jesus speaking the psalm. The Gospels report that Jesus would make the psalms his own at crucial moments in his life. For example, as he hung on the cross, he cried out in the words of Psalm 22, "My God, my God, why have you forsaken me?" (Matt. 27:46, citing Ps. 22:1). In the gospel of John, the narrator cites Psalm 69 as if Jesus is speaking it in the context of cleansing the temple (see John 2:17, citing Ps. 69:9).

Special consideration may be given to the kingship psalms in relationship to Jesus. Psalm 2 is an especially well-known example, cited frequently in the New Testament in relationship to Christ (Mark 1:11 [and parallels]; 9:7 [and parallels]; Acts 4:23 – 31; 13:33; Rom. 1:4; Heb. 1:5; 5:5; 2 Peter 1:17; Rev. 11:18; 19:19). During the Old Testament period, this psalm was almost certainly a coronation psalm sung at the inauguration of a new king in the dynasty of David. After all, in verse 7 the author cites 2 Samuel 7:14 ("I will be his father, and he will be my son") in the context of the covenant that God made with David with the promise that "your house and your kingdom will endure forever before me; your throne will be established forever" (7:16). However, in 586 BC Babylon brought the Davidic dynasty to an end. After this moment and into the future there was no human descendant of David on the throne in Jerusalem. This crisis caused faithful readers during the intertestamental period to recognize that there was a deeper meaning than they had thought previously. The New Testament authors saw Jesus as the fulfillment of this promise.

Recommended Resources

Allender, D., and T. Longman. *Cry of the Soul.* Colorado Springs: NavPress, 1994.

Broyles, C. *Psalms.* NIBCOT. Peabody, MA: Hendrickson, 1999.

Brueggemann, W. *The Message of the Psalms.* Minneapolis: Augsburg, 1984.

Firth, D., and P. S. Johnston, eds. *Interpreting the Psalms: Issues and Approaches.* Downers Grove, IL: InterVarsity Press, 2005.

Goldingay, J. *Psalms 1 – 41.* BCOTWP. Grand Rapids: Baker, 2006.

____. *Psalms 42 – 89.* BCOTWP. Grand Rapids: Baker, 2007.

_____. *Psalms 90–150*. BCOTWP. Grand Rapids: Baker, 2008.

Kidner, D. *Psalms*. TOTC. Downers Grove, IL: InterVarsity Press, 1973.

Longman, T. *How to Read the Psalms*. Downers Grove, IL: InterVarsity Press, 1987.

Miller, Jr., P. D. *Interpreting the Psalms*. Minneapolis: Fortress, 1986.

Wilson, G. H. *Psalms*. Vol. 1. NIVAC. Grand Rapids: Zondervan, 2002.

Questions for Review and Discussion

1. What is the significance of the division of the book of Psalms into five books?

2. No psalms embed the specific occasion that led to its composition in the body of the song. How does that enable later worshipers to use the Psalms as a "mirror of their soul"?

3. Martin Luther called the book of Psalms a "fair pleasure garden." What do you think he meant by this?

4. Read Psalm 110. How do you think this psalm was read during the Old Testament time period? How is it read after the coming of Christ?

5. What are the characteristics of Hebrew poetry?

6. Look at Psalm 2:1–6 and discuss the parallelism.

7. Psalm 78:65 presents a striking image of God: "Then the Lord awoke as from sleep, as a warrior wakes from the stupor of wine." Discuss what this image intends to communicate about God.

8. Read Psalm 130 and discuss its genre.

chapter seventeen

THE BOOK
OF PROVERBS

Content: What Is Proverbs About?

The preamble to Proverbs (1:1–7) states that the book is about *wisdom*, a full description of which is given below. The preamble not only tells us about the purpose of the book, but also names an author and the audience.

The first part of Proverbs (1:8–9:18) is composed of about sixteen discourses or speeches. Most of these speeches are lectures of a father to his son (1:8–19; 2:1–22; 3:13–20; 3:21–35; 4:1–9; 4:10–19; 4:20–27; 5:1–23; 6:1–19; 6:20–35; 7:1–27; 9:7–12). These lectures include strong exhortations to pursue wisdom. They speak of the benefits of wisdom and the dangers of folly. In these speeches the father puts a special emphasis on the need for the son to avoid promiscuous women. The father likens life to a "path." Everyone is on a path, but the path is either a straight, well-lit one that leads to life or a twisty, dark one that is strewn with traps, nets, and snares and leads to death. The purpose of the father's teaching is to keep the son on the former path, the path of wisdom.

The other speeches in this first section of Proverbs are words from a woman called Wisdom (1:20–33; 8:1–36; 9:1–6), in contrast to the speech of Woman Folly (9:13–18). Woman Wisdom speaks to all the young men. Her significance in the book of Proverbs is addressed below.

The second and longer part of Proverbs (chaps. 10–31) is composed mainly of proverbs, the literary form that gives its name to the book. (The Hebrew name *Meshalim* is typically translated

"Proverbs.") Proverbs are short observations, admonitions, or prohibitions. A fuller description of a proverb will be given below.
Contrary to the opinion of some, the proverbs do not seem to be sys-
tematically arranged by theme or by any other device like catchwords
or sound patterns. They are random reflections on the randomness of
life. Thus the main themes or topics of the book appear sporadically
throughout the collection and include wealth and poverty, speech,
laziness, authority, sexuality, family relationships, alcohol, self-con-
trol, planning for the future, and bribes/gifts. These topics touch on
the nitty-gritty of life and intend to keep a person on the path of life
and help them avoid the path that leads to death. The book ends with
a relatively long poem on the virtuous woman (31:10 – 31).

Many Christians use the book of Proverbs as an anthology of
"mottos," providing guidelines for good behavior. On a more sophis-
ticated level, Proverbs is often used as a sourcebook for biblical coun-
seling. However, two pitfalls must be avoided: (1) the tendency to
absolutize the proverbs, and (2) reading the proverbs in an isolated
and abstract manner. The individual proverbs must be interpreted
and applied within the context of the whole book and, indeed, of the
whole Bible. They are not divine promises for the here and now, but
true observations that time will bear out.

Authorship: Who Wrote Proverbs?

The book begins by apparently naming Solomon, the third king of Israel
(965 – 928 BC), as the author (1:1). The historical books paint a portrait
of Solomon as a king of uncommon wisdom given to him by God (see
1 Kings 3:1 – 15). He demonstrated his wisdom by the insight of his decision making (1 Kings 3:16 – 28). Indeed, he is said to have written over
three thousand proverbs (1 Kings 4:32)—far more than in the book of
Proverbs—and his wisdom is said to be "greater than the wisdom of
all the people of the East, and greater than all the wisdom of Egypt"
(1 Kings 4:30). Moreover, the story of the Queen of Sheba indicates that
Solomon's wisdom was "world famous." Since Solomon is also famous
for his slide into folly through his love of foreign women, his composition
of Proverbs is traditionally assigned to the maturity of his reign.

While there is no good reason to doubt that Solomon wrote proverbs that are included in the book, there is also indisputable evidence
that other authors and editors contributed to the final form of the book.

In the first place, we should note that twice (22:17; 24:23) a significant section of the book (22:17 – 24:34) is ascribed to a group

simply known as "the wise." Proverbs 30:1 and 31:1 name Agur and Lemuel respectively as authors. Interestingly, Proverbs 10:1 names Solomon as composer of the section that follows (raising the question whether the material in 9:8–9:18 is Solomonic), as does 25:1. The latter reference is particularly interesting in that it says that this Solomonic material was added to the book (and edited?) by the men of Hezekiah who lived about two centuries after Solomon.

We end up with the following picture of an anthology of wisdom materials collected over a number of centuries:

Preamble, of unknown authorship but probably a late editor (1:1–7)

Extended Discourses on Wisdom, anonymous, perhaps Solomonic (1:8–9:18)

Solomonic Proverbs (10:1–22:16; 25:1–29:27)

Sayings of the Wise (22:17–24:34)

Sayings of Agur (30:1–33)

Sayings of King Lemuel (31:1–9)

Poem to the Virtuous Woman, anonymous (31:10–31)

Date: When Was Proverbs Written?

Proverbs was written over an undetermined but long period of time. If we take seriously the book's connection with Solomon, that would date an early form of the book to the mid-tenth century BC. Of course, Solomon may have collected individual proverbs that predated that time. The only other concrete historical reference in the book is to the "men of Hezekiah," who added more proverbs of Solomon to the collection (25:1), and this expansion of the book would have taken place then in the late eighth to early seventh century BC. The "words of the wise" and the sayings of Agur and Lemuel are undated. The appearance of the book in the third part of the Hebrew canon (the Writings) may suggest that the book was not finally completed until the exilic or postexilic period. The exact date of the book is not important for its interpretation.

Genre: What Style of Literature Is Proverbs?

Proverbs is wisdom literature, which seeks to impart a skill of living with a foundation on the "fear of the LORD." The first nine chapters are made up of discourses or speeches of a father to a son (e.g., 1:8–19) or of a woman named Wisdom to all the young men (e.g., chap. 8).

The second part is made up of proverbs, which are brief observations, admonitions, or prohibitions about life. Proverbs are only true if applied to the right situation. For instance, Proverbs 26:4 ("Do not answer a fool according to his folly ...") and 26:5 ("Answer a fool according to his folly ...") are both true if applied to the right situation. A wise person will not only know the proverbs but know how to use them (26:7, 9). The wisdom of the proverbs is often encouraged by good outcomes associated with right action and speech and negative outcomes with wrong actions and speech. For instance, "Lazy hands make for poverty, but diligent hands bring wealth" (10:4). However, these rewards and punishments are not promises or guarantees, but the expected outcome, all other factors being equal. They encourage behavior that is the best route to a desired conclusion.

Connections: How Does Proverbs Anticipate the Gospel?

One starting point for relating the theology of Proverbs to the theology of the New Testament is Jesus' being associated with the figure of Wisdom. For instance, when Paul writes, "The Son is the image of the invisible God, the firstborn over all creation" (Col. 1:15), he is using language from Proverbs 8. Similarly, Revelation 3:14, which refers to Jesus as "the ruler of God's creation," evokes the picture of Wisdom's role at creation. At one point, Jesus himself draws the connection. When his behavior angered his opponents, he responded by saying, "Wisdom is proved right by her deeds" (Matt. 11:19). Jesus embodies the wisdom of God. God's wisdom is one of Jesus' most frequently mentioned traits in the New Testament. Jesus is the wisdom of God (1 Cor. 1:30), the one "in whom are hidden all the treasures of wisdom and knowledge" (Col. 2:3). During his earthly ministry, Jesus' wisdom was revealed through his teaching (Mark 1:22; Luke 2:41–50, 52). His predominant teaching form was the parable, a wisdom form.

Recommended Resources

Fox, M. *Proverbs 1–9.* AB. New Haven: Yale University Press, 2000.
_____. *Proverbs 10–31.* AB. New Haven: Yale University Press, 2009.
Longman, T. *How to Read Proverbs.* Downers Grove, IL: InterVarsity Press, 2002.

_____. *Proverbs*. BCOTWP. Baker, 2006.

_____. "Proverbs." Pages 466–503 in ZIBBC 5. Edited by J. H. Walton. Grand Rapids: Zondervan, 2009.

Waltke, B. K. *Proverbs*. 2 vols. NICOT. Grand Rapids: Eerdmans, 2004–5.

Questions for Review and Discussion

1. Who wrote Proverbs?
2. What is wisdom?
3. Who is Woman Wisdom? Woman Folly? What is the contribution of chapter 9 to the message of the book of Proverbs?
4. What is a proverb? How should we interpret and understand proverbs?
5. Are proverbs promises? Why or why not?
6. Are proverbs always true?
7. How is Christ related to Woman Wisdom?

chapter eighteen

THE BOOK
OF ECCLESIASTES

Content: What Is Ecclesiastes About?

Ecclesiastes contains the message of "the Teacher," traditionally the preacher, who writes in the first person in 1:12–12:7, as well as that of a second unnamed wisdom teacher, whose words frame the Teacher's in 1:1–11 and 12:8–14. The Teacher speaks in the first person ("I, the Teacher"), while the second wise teacher speaks about the Teacher ("The Teacher, he"). The unnamed wisdom teacher, who may be called the frame narrator, introduces and comments on the words of the Teacher to his son (12:12). Thus, in order to understand the book of Ecclesiastes, the reader must understand the message of the Teacher and also the evaluation of that message by the frame narrator.

The message of the Teacher is "life is difficult and then you die." Famously, he repeats the word "meaningless" more than forty times to drive home his message that there is no ultimate purpose to life. He relates how he tried to find meaning in work (2:18–23; 4:4–6), pleasure (2:1–11), wealth (5:10–6:9), wisdom (2:12–17), and power (4:13–16). Each time he concludes that there is no meaning. Death (12:1–7), the inability to discern the right time to do the right thing (3:1–15), and injustice (3:16–22; 7:15–18; 8:10–15) are the reasons why life makes no sense to him. What, then, should a person do in the light of the ultimate meaninglessness of life? *Carpe diem!* ("Seize the day!") Six times in the book the Teacher advocates small pleasures like eating and drinking in order to distract oneself from the harsh realities of life and the inevitability of death (2:24–26; 3:12–14, 22; 5:18–20; 8:15; 9:7–10).

The Teacher's conclusions, however, are not the final message of the book of Ecclesiastes, which is associated with the evaluation of the frame narrator. In his preamble (1:2–11) the frame narrator simply sets the mood for the Teacher's difficult teaching, but in the epilogue (12:8–14) he responds to the Teacher's viewpoint and sets his son in a positive direction. In his evaluation, he affirms the truth of the Teacher's perspective; it is true that if we accept the Teacher's "under the sun" viewpoint (that is, trying to find meaning apart from God), we will conclude that life is meaningless. However, the narrator does not stop there. He gives his son an "above the sun" perspective in the last two verses, when he tells him to "fear God and keep his commandments, for this is the duty of all mankind. For God will bring every deed into judgment, including every hidden thing, whether it is good or evil" (12:13–14). In short compass, the narrator tells his son to adopt the proper attitude toward God characterized by fear (see Prov. 1:7) and to maintain his relationship with God by keeping the law and by expecting the future judgment.

Authorship and Date: Who Wrote Ecclesiastes and When?

On the basis of the superscription (1:1) — which associates the Teacher with a "son of David, king in Jerusalem" — the traditional view is that Solomon wrote the book, though there is no direct statement that he did. Indeed, the author of the book would more likely be identified with the frame narrator, who was writing about the Teacher. The association between the Teacher and King Solomon was probably to remind the reader about someone who had more wealth, wisdom, power, and pleasure than anyone else, but who was still not able to find meaning in it. He was a man who at the end of his life did not put God first, and thus he was responsible for the division of Israel into two kingdoms. In the final analysis, it is best to conclude that we do not know who the author of the book is, though the subject matter indicates that it was a product of the intellectual elite.

If the traditional ascription to Solomon is correct, then it was written during his reign (965–928 BC), probably toward the end of his life. If the book is anonymous, we cannot be certain when it was written. Most scholars who study the book would date it relatively late in the Old Testament time period, during either the Persian period (539–331 BC) or even the Greek period (sometime after 331 BC) because the Teacher's thinking reflects the philosophical currents of those days.

Genre: What Style of Literature Is Ecclesiastes?

We have already identified Ecclesiastes as a wisdom book (see Proverbs). The style of the Teacher's speech (1:12–12:7) is similar to ancient Near Eastern autobiographies, especially those that contain lessons derived from the speaker's life experiences (Cuthaean Legend of Naram-Sin; Adad-guppi autobiography; the Sin of Sargon text). Yet the book as a whole contains more than this autobiography, since it is framed by the words of the narrator. Thus Ecclesiastes is a framed wisdom autobiography.

Connections: How Does Ecclesiastes Anticipate the Gospel?

In Romans 8:18–20 Paul writes, "I consider that our present sufferings are not worth comparing with the glory that will be revealed in us. For the creation waits in eager expectation for the children of God to be revealed. For the creation was subjected to *frustration*. . . ." It is notable that the Greek word here translated "frustration" (*mataiotes*) is the same word used to translate the Hebrew word "meaningless" (*hebel*) in the Greek translation of Ecclesiastes. Paul almost certainly knew that he was making this allusion, even though he is also referring back to Genesis 3, where God subjected the world to frustration in response to the rebellion of his human creatures. In other words, the Teacher is frustrated because he is trying to find meaning in a fallen world.

Paul, however, is not frustrated. He continues by saying that God subjected the world to frustration "in hope" of redemption (8:20–25). He knows that Jesus Christ subjected himself to the fallen, meaningless world in order to free us from its curse (Gal. 3:13; Phil. 2:6–8). Jesus even died on the cross, experiencing death—which was a chief cause of the Teacher's belief that life was meaningless—defeating death, and freeing us from its victory over us (1 Cor. 15:50–57). In Christ, who defeated death by his resurrection, we know that our "labor in the Lord is not in vain" (1 Cor. 15:58).

Recommended Resources

Allender, D., and T. Longman. *Breaking the Idols of Your Heart: How to Navigate the Temptations of Life.* Downers Grove, IL: InterVarsity Press, 2007.

Bartholomew, C. G. *Ecclesiastes.* BCOTWP. Grand Rapids: Baker, 2009.

Longman, T. *Ecclesiastes*. NICOT. Grand Rapids: Eerdmans, 1998.
_____. "Ecclesiastes." Pages 251–337 in *Job, Ecclesiastes, Song of Songs*. CsBC. Carol Stream, IL: Tyndale House, 2006.
Provan, I. *Ecclesiastes, Song of Songs*. NIVAC. Grand Rapids: Zondervan, 2001.
Shepherd, J. E. "Ecclesiastes." Pages 253–365 in *Proverbs–Isaiah*. EBC-R 6. Grand Rapids: Zondervan, 2008.

Questions for Review and Discussion

1. What is the primary theme of the book of Ecclesiastes? How does that theme relate to your own life?
2. Explain how the two speakers in the book interact with each other. What message does each have, and which is the final conclusion of the book?
3. What can we say about the authorship of the book and the date it was written? Does it make any difference to our interpretation of the message of the book? Why or why not?
4. How does the book of Ecclesiastes anticipate Jesus Christ?

chapter nineteen

THE BOOK OF SONG OF SONGS

Content: What Is the Song of Songs About?

The Song is about the love between a man and a woman. The book celebrates such love through poems that in turn express a desire for physical intimacy. The book is a collection of a little over twenty love poems (see Genre below); some are spoken by the man to the woman, and some are the woman lovingly addressing the man. The Song does not tell a story, but rather expresses deep desire through the use of vivid and sometimes provocative imagery. Besides a celebration, the Song warns young women (represented by the Chorus, the Daughters of Jerusalem) not to hurry into a passionate relationship, but to wait until the time is right (2:7; 3:5; 8:4).

Authorship and Date: Who Wrote the Song of Songs and When?

The superscription (1:1) associates the Song with Solomon, who reigned as king of Israel from 965 to 928 BC. It is possible that Solomon wrote some of the poems that constitute the Song of Songs and thus is the fountainhead of its composition. However, the role that Solomon plays within the Song and the fact that the historical Solomon was a negative example in the area of love and marriage (1 Kings 11:1) make it unlikely that he wrote the whole book. Like Proverbs, the Song is most likely an anthology of love poems written by a number of people, though there likely was a final, anonymous editor who placed the Song in its final form.

If it was written by Solomon, then he did it in the tenth century BC, but it is more likely that the Song is a collection of love poems that achieved its final form at a later point in Israel's history.

Genre: What Style of Literature Is the Song of Songs?

The identification of the genre of the Song of Songs is pivotal for its correct interpretation and application. For centuries the Song was thought to be an allegory of the love between God and Israel or between God and the church. God was thought to be the man, and Israel the woman (in Jewish interpretation) or the church (or perhaps the individual believer, in Christian interpretation). The arbitrary nature of this allegorical interpretation led to its abandonment in the nineteenth century, though some sermons may still be heard in this vein.

The vast majority of Protestant, Catholic, and Jewish interpreters today understand the Song as love poetry. Some believe it tells the story of a couple moving from courtship to marriage to honeymoon. A variation on this "dramatic approach" to the Song takes the story to be about a love triangle, with a king (perhaps Solomon) taking a young woman into his harem, yet she remains in love with the shepherd boy back home.

Proponents of an anthological approach argue that one must read too much into the poetry to create a story, and they prefer the view that the Song is a collection of love poems. They consider it literally a single song composed of multiple songs.

Whether it is a drama or a collection of poems, the Song contains beautiful, sensuous poetry that expresses passionate emotions through the use of evocative imagery.

The purpose of the Song is, first, to celebrate physical intimacy between a man and a woman. In this regard, the garden settings of a number of the poems are significant. God created Adam and Eve and placed them in a garden, where they were "both naked, and they felt no shame" (Gen. 2:25). Due to their rebellion and alienation from God, the harmony that they experienced in their relationship with each other was also broken. God removed them from the garden, and they put on clothes, representing their estrangement. In the Song, a man and the woman are in the garden again, enjoying their relationship with each other, indicating that a healthy and enjoyable relationship is possible.

Even so, the Song also signals that such a relationship is not easy and often runs into problems. Certain poems (see especially 5:2 – 6:3) describe how intimacy is difficult as the man moves toward the woman and the woman moves away, and when the woman moves toward the man, the man moves away. Eventually the woman searches for the man by moving through difficult obstacles (represented by the "watchmen," 3:3; 5:7) and finally is reunited with him in the garden of love.

In these poems the poet paints a picture of the already/not yet redemption of sexuality. It describes a relationship that is mutual, intimate, passionate, and exclusive. While the man and woman are not often explicitly described as married (though see the marriage language at 3:6 – 11; 4:10 – 11), there is no question — based on the fact that the Song is in the context of the canon — that the assumption is that these are poems expressing the desires of a married couple.

Reading the Song within the canon also leads to another theological dimension of the book. One of the most powerful metaphors of God's relationship with his people is that of marriage and the intimate relationship of a husband (representing God) and a wife (representing his people; see, for example, Ezek. 16, 23 and Hosea 1 and 3). Thus the more we learn about the relationship of the man and the woman, the more we learn about our relationship with God, in particular that it should be mutual, intimate, passionate, and exclusive.

Connections: How Does the Song of Songs Anticipate the Gospel?

The Song is about the intimate relationship of a man and a woman. In the previous section we observed that the marriage metaphor is a frequent one to help people understand the mutual, intimate, passionate, exclusive relationship that they have with God. Paul uses this metaphor of marriage in Ephesians 5:21 – 33 to describe the Christian's relationship with Jesus Christ. Thus the Song as it describes the relationship between the man and the woman inspires us to think about the intimacy we enjoy with Jesus.

Recommended Resources

Allender, D. B., and T. Longman. *Intimate Allies*. Wheaton, IL: Tyndale House, 1995.

Exum, C. J. *Song of Songs*. OTL. Louisville, KY: Westminster John Knox, 2005.

Hess, R. R. *Song of Songs*. BCOTWP. Grand Rapids: Baker, 2005.

Longman, T. "Song of Songs." Pages 239–93 in *Job, Ecclesiastes, Song of Songs*. CsBC. Carol Stream, IL: Tyndale House, 2006.

_____. *Song of Songs*. NICOT. Grand Rapids: Eerdmans, 2001.

Questions for Review and Discussion

1. How would you describe the Song of Songs—an allegory, a drama, love poems? Why?
2. What is Solomon's connection to the Song of Songs?
3. How does the genre of the Song of Songs affect interpretation?
4. What value do you think the Song of Songs has for the church today?
5. What can a Christian reader learn about God from the Song of Songs?
6. How do you think the Song of Songs contributes to the message of the Bible as a whole?

chapter twenty

THE BOOK OF ISAIAH

Content: What Is Isaiah About?

The book of Isaiah contains prophetic oracles as well as narratives that speak to Isaiah's immediate historical situation in the eighth century BC and beyond, the latter raising the question of the authorial unity of the book (see below). In addition, the book presents narratives about Isaiah and his contemporaries. While the structure of the book is complex, its broad outlines can be clearly seen.

The first part of the book is largely taken up with issues of the immediate present and impending judgment on Israel (chaps. 1–12). This portion is then followed by an extended series of oracles focusing on judgment against the foreign nations (chaps. 13–35). The remainder of the book is given to describing future blessing for the people of God (chaps. 40–66). Chapters 36–39 provide a narrative transition from the time of the Assyrian crisis to the concerns of the exilic and later times.

While Jeremiah and Ezekiel begin with accounts of their call to the prophetic ministry, the book of Isaiah starts with a series of oracles that highlight the main themes of the book—divine judgment for Israel's sins as well as future hope that will follow that judgment (chaps. 1–5). The opening oracle illustrates the concerns of this first section of the book: 1:2–17 enumerates the sins of God's people that deserve judgment, and verses 18–20 present the alternatives of repentance and restoration or rejection and destruction. The remainder of the chapter returns to a description of the corruption of the people and then to their future restoration due to God's purging of their sin. In this basic message Isaiah is similar to the other prophets of the Bible. After presenting the message of judgment and hope, we hear of Isaiah's commission by God in the divine throne room, represented by the temple itself (chap. 6). Isaiah readily agrees to be God's spokesperson, and his lips are cleansed by the touch of a coal from the altar fires.

The next major section of the book (chaps. 7–12) is deeply rooted in the historical events of Isaiah's time. Syria ruled by Rezin and Israel ruled by Pekah threaten to attack Judah and its king, Ahaz, for refusing to join them in an alliance against an expanding Assyria under Tiglath-pileser III. Isaiah encourages Ahaz that God will not let them harm Judah, but also admonishes him not to enter into an alliance with the Assyrians. He even provides a sign to Ahaz to credential his prophetic message, the birth of a child given the name Immanuel ("God is with us") to a virgin (7:14). The context makes it clear that the (first) fulfillment of this prophetic word would come soon, and by the time the child was old enough to reject the wrong and choose the right, the threat from these kings would be gone. Powerful pictures of a future bright with hope under the leadership of a future messiah (9:1–7; 11) fill this section of Isaiah.

In spite of Isaiah's warnings, the historical books inform us that Ahaz did indeed call on the Assyrian king and, although Tiglath-pileser prevented Rezin and Pekah from moving against Judah, Judah was from that moment on a vassal of Assyria (2 Kings 16). Ahaz failed God by relying on a powerful foreign nation, Assyria.

The next major section of the book (chaps. 13–23) contains a series of oracles against the foreign nations (Babylon, Assyria, Philistia, Moab, Damascus, Cush, Egypt, Babylon [a second time], Edom, Arabia, and Tyre). The implicit message concerning Ahaz's decision is that he is trusting in nations that God will soon overturn. God is not just the God of Israel and Judah, but the God of the whole world. He holds the nations accountable for their crimes as well as his own people. This message of Isaiah's is similar to those of many other prophets, including Jeremiah (chaps. 46–51), Ezekiel (chaps. 21–32), Obadiah, and Nahum.

These oracles against the foreign nations lead naturally to the next section (chaps. 24–27), an announcement of judgment against the whole earth. The prophet begins with a powerful description of God's future devastation of the entire world. On the one hand, the city that represents the wicked will be ruined (24:10, 12; 25:2–3, 12;

27:10). People's happy songs will come to an end (24:8–9; 25:5). On the other hand, God's redeemed people will sing joyful songs (24:14, 16; 26:1, 19; 27:2) in God's city (25:6, 9; 26:1). While "the new wine dries up and the vine withers" (24:7) for the wicked, God prepares "a feast of rich food for all peoples, a banquet of aged wine" (25:6) for his people on the mountain of the Lord. In that future day, God will slay Leviathan, an ancient Near Eastern symbol of evil (27:1), and bring deliverance to his people.

Chapters 28–33 continue the issue of trust. Chapters 28–29 start with oracles against Israel and Judah. The leaders have let God's people down by their sin. Chapters 30–31 castigate them for putting their dependence on Egypt, while chapters 32–33 look to a king who will rule with righteousness. Chapters 34–35 then bring the issue to a point that those who trust in the nations will become like a wilderness, while those who trust God will be like a wilderness that is turned into a garden.

The final part of the first major portion of the book (chaps. 36–39) brings the theme of trust in God rather than the nations to an interesting climax. While earlier (chaps. 7–12) we have a historical narrative of Ahaz during the Syro-Ephraimite war, showing a king who trusted the nations rather than God, here we have the story of a king, Hezekiah, who, though tempted, listens to Isaiah and trusts God. This latter story is set during the incursion of King Sennacherib of Assyria in 701 BC, and the result of Hezekiah's faith is the withdrawal of the attacking army. That Hezekiah is not perfect (and thus not the messiah) is the point of chapter 39, when he shows his treasures to Merodach-baladan of Babylon, indicating a willingness to ally with him against Assyria. Isaiah announces that punishment will not come immediately, but in the future, when Babylon, rather than Assyria, will pillage his descendants. In this anticipation of the future role of the Babylonians, these chapters also function as a transition to the second major part of the book.

While the first part of the book is predominantly focused on judgment, the second half is mainly concerned with hope and future redemption. The implied setting of the oracles of chapters 40–55 is the Babylonian exile. The prophet begins by anticipating the people's deliverance from exile as an analogy with the entry into the land from the wilderness after the exodus from Egypt (40:1–5). The idea of deliverance from exile is a major concern of this part of Isaiah, including even the mention of Cyrus the king of Persia, who is called God's anointed (messiah), who will rescue them from the Babylonians (44:24–45:13). In order to keep God's people on the right track, the prophet also makes a strong contrast between the idols of the nations and the true God (43:8–44:28). Indeed, God will save Judah from Babylon and its false gods (46:1–48:12).

The most memorable picture that emerges from these chapters, though, is the description of the servant of the Lord (42:1–9; 49:1–6; 50:4–6; 52:13–53:12). Who is the servant? In the original context, there can be little question that Isaiah's servant is to be identified as Israel; the servant is specifically called "my servant Israel/Jacob" (41:8–9; 44:1–2, 21; 45:4; 48:20; 49:3–6). It is because the faithful remnant rises from a period of judgment that surviving Israel can be called the "Suffering Servant." God has been with them through the fire and through the deep (43:1–2), and now he will make "little Israel" strong again (41:8–14). His servant will be righteous and will bring justice to the nations (42:1–9). God will bring his people from the ends of the earth to be his witnesses, his servants (43:5–13). He will pour out his Spirit on the offspring of the servant of the Lord, and they will flourish like grass in a meadow (44:1–4). Though the nation has sinned, this surviving remnant-servant will be faithful.

While chapters 1–39 are set during the time of the historical Isaiah and look forward to the immediate future, and chapters 40–55 are set in the context of the Babylonian exile and look forward to future release and restoration, the final chapters (56–66) are set during the restoration. Problems remain, including corrupt leaders (blind watchmen; 56:9–57:2), hypocritical worship (58:1–14), and continued idolatry (57:3–13). Chapter 59 confesses that Israel's continued struggles are not God's fault, but are due to the continued sin of the people. Yet the restoration from exile was just the beginning. Isaiah looks forward to an even greater future described as new heavens and a new earth (chaps. 65–66).

Authorship and Date: Who Wrote Isaiah and When?

The question of the authorship of Isaiah is hotly contested. The traditional approach takes the superscription (1:1) at face value and as extending to the whole book. The superscription names Isaiah son of Amoz, a prophet of the eighth and early seventh centuries BC, as the origin of the oracles that are found in the book.

There are some reasons to think that Isaiah of Amoz was not the author of the whole book. While such thinking arose within the context of historical criticism, today many evangelical scholars agree that Isaiah did not write the entire book. The latter do not deny the supernatural character of prophecy, but argue that the second part of the book is prophecy that is set at a later period of time. In other words, Isaiah 40 and following are the words of a prophet who is living during the Babylonian exile and from that vantage point anticipates deliverance (40:9–11; 42:1–9; 43:1–7; 44:24–28; 48:12–22; 49:8–23; 51:11; 52:1–12) and judgment against their captors (43:14–15; 47:1–15; 48:14; 49:24–26; 51:21–23). King Cyrus of Persia is within the immediate foreview of the prophet and is mentioned by name (44:28; 45:1, 13). Some experts in Isaiah differentiate Isaiah 40–55 from 56–66 on the same grounds, since the latter finds its setting at an ever later period of time, the Persian period. Of course, many other factors are brought to bear on this question. For instance, it is commonly pointed out that while the first part ("first Isaiah") speaks of a future messianic king (9:6–7; 11:1–11), the second part ("second Isaiah") does not, but rather describes the suffering servant, who is not mentioned in the first part. Differences in language and style are also marshaled to make this argument, but such arguments are precarious at best, since such changes can be explained by a change of topic rather than a change of author. Indeed, today, even among those who affirm multiple authorship, there is an emphasis on the thematic unity of the book.

Advocates of Isaianic authorship of the whole also point to New Testament citations of the book, which occur some twenty times. John, for instance, cites 6:10 and 53:1 in contiguous verses (John 12:38, 40), identifying both as Isaiah: "Isaiah said this because he saw Jesus' glory and spoke about him" (v. 41).

The authorship of Isaiah is one of the more difficult questions of Old Testament study. The most compelling argument in favor of multiple Isaiahs is the multiple settings and putative audiences in the eighth century (chaps. 1–39, for the most part), the Babylonian exile (chaps. 40–55), and the Persian period (chaps. 56–66), but a possible rejoinder is that the prophet is employing an event vision and thus speaking as if he is living during those time periods. In other words, it is a literary device that gives the prophecy a sense of vividness and urgency. The strongest argument in favor of the traditional argument is the superscription and no indication of a change of author throughout. The idea that a second unnamed prophet—perhaps someone who saw himself as a disciple of Isaiah—simply appended his oracles to the great master seems out of keeping with the nature of ancient prophecy, where, contrary to most writing, authorship is an important matter.

That being said, the issue of the authorship of the book is so complex it should not be made a test for orthodoxy. In some respect, the end results of the debate are somewhat irrelevant: whether written by Isaiah in the eighth century or others who applied his insights to a later time, Isaiah 40–66 clearly was addressed in large measure to the needs of the exilic community.

Genre: What Style of Literature Is Isaiah?

The book of Isaiah contains mostly poetic oracles but also narratives about Isaiah (see, for instance, chaps. 6–8 and 36–39). The oracles are both judgment oracles (the emphasis in chaps. 1–39) and salvation oracles (the emphasis in chaps. 40–66). Subcategories of judgment and salvation oracles include a love song that functions like a parable (5:1–7), woe oracles that mimic a funeral dirge (29:1–12), hymns of praise (12:1–6), messianic prophecies (9:1–7; 11:1–9), and servant songs (42:1–9). The poetry of Isaiah is among the richest and most profound in the Hebrew Bible.

Connections: How Does Isaiah Anticipate the Gospel?

Isaiah is one of the most quoted books in the New Testament. Only a few examples may be given here to demonstrate the importance of the witness of Isaiah to the gospel. The gospel writers saw in the virgin birth of Christ a heightened and intensified fulfillment of Isaiah's words in 7:14, that Christ indeed is "God with us" (Immanuel; see Matt. 1:23). Isaiah anticipated a second Exodus, a salvation event that would exceed the one from the time of Moses. It would be preceded by a voice in the wilderness (40:3), who turns out to be John the Baptist (Matt. 3:3; Luke 3:4–6; John 1:23). The gospel writers also cite Isaiah 6:9–10 to explain why Jesus taught in parables and was not understood by those who listened to him (Matt. 13:13–15; 15:7–9; John 12:39–40; Acts 28:24–27).

While, as mentioned above, in the original context the suffering servant was the righteous remnant of Israel, the New Testament writers perceived that Isaiah's description went beyond the nation of Israel. Isaiah individualized this servant: he is born of a woman, and he comes as one who is distinct from the nation, one who will restore the tribes of Jacob and bring back Israel (44:24; 46:3; 49:1). The remnant community in the restoration period did not live up to Isaiah's lofty goal of being a purified nation. Thus Christian readers can understand how the New Testament writers were following the lead of Isaiah himself. In their eyes, Jesus had become a remnant of one. He was the embodiment of faithful Israel, the truly righteous and suffering servant (see Isa. 51:1, cited in John 12:38; Acts 8:27–33; and Isa. 53:3, cited in Matt. 8:17).

In addition, Isaiah anticipates Jesus' mission to the Gentiles (9:1–12, cited in Matt. 4:13–16). Jesus was the servant in Isaiah who was called to the vulnerable (61:1–3, cited in Luke 4:14–21). Paul cites 11:10 (in Rom. 15:12) and 65:1 (in Rom. 10:20) to justify the inclusion of the Gentiles in the church.

Recommended Resources

Goldingay, J. *Isaiah*. NIBCOT. Peabody, MA: Hendrickson, 2001.
Motyer, A. *Isaiah*. Leicester, UK: Inter-Varsity Press, 1999.
Oswalt, J. N. *Isaiah*. NIVAC. Grand Rapids: Zondervan, 2003.

Questions for Reflection and Discussion

1. What are the issues involved in determining the authorship of Isaiah?
2. How does Ahaz respond to Isaiah's call to trust in the Lord?
3. How do the oracles against the foreign nations fit into Isaiah's message?
4. Describe the structure of the book of Isaiah.
5. Describe how Isaiah connects to the Syro-Ephraimite war.
6. Name the ways in which the gospel writers appropriate the message of Isaiah.

chapter twenty-one

THE BOOK
OF JEREMIAH

Content: What Is Jeremiah About?

Jeremiah is the longest book by word count in the entire Bible. That said, its main message is capable of brief restatement. The prophet speaks on behalf of God in charging Judah with violation of the covenant they made with God on Mount Sinai. Initially he calls on them to repent, but when they fail to do so, he announces the coming judgment, which takes the form of the Babylonian invasion. Jeremiah not only preaches this message, but also supports the message by performing various sign acts. Judgment is not Jeremiah's only message, however. He also delivers salvation oracles, indicating that God is not yet done with Judah and Jerusalem.

Jeremiah is a prophet not only to the people of God, but also to the nations (1:10), so he also speaks oracles and performs sign acts concerning the nations that surround Judah. In addition to the prophetic oracles and sign acts, the book contains stories about Jeremiah as well as his complaints. We can offer only a few examples of these various elements of the book as we survey its structure.

As is typical of prophetic books, Jeremiah does not have a tight organization, but like many prophets begins with a superscription (1:1–3, discussed below under Authorship and Date) and then follows it with an account of Jeremiah's divine call to prophetic ministry (1:4–10). Though he protests that he is but a youth (evoking the memory of Moses' reluctance to be a prophet), God insists that he will be with him and take care of him. Then God touches his mouth (evoking the memory of Isaiah's prophetic call, Isa. 6:6–7) as he tells Jeremiah to speak both judgment and salvation to Judah and the nations. The first chapter concludes with two short initial oracles, announcing that God will watch to make sure his word will be fulfilled and also that judgment is coming from the north (1:11 – 19). As time proceeds, it becomes clear that this is an initial reference to a Babylonian invasion of Judah.

Jeremiah 2 – 24 is a collection of sermons, poetic and prose oracles, and prophetic sign acts that are undated. Indeed, it is often difficult to tell when one oracle ends and another begins. These oracles charge Judah with breaking God's covenant, particularly by their idolatry. The oracle found in 11:1 – 17 accuses Israel of breaking the Mosaic covenant and warns them that the curses of that covenant are about to be unleashed. The hope is that the people will repent. The oracle in 10:1 – 6 specifically charges them with idolatry, and other oracles cite other violations of God's law, such as lying, deception, and fraud (9:2 – 6); oppression of the vulnerable, such as foreigners, widows, and orphans (7:6); breaking the Sabbath (19:19 – 27) — which after all is the sign of the Mosaic covenant (Exod. 31:12 – 18) — and many other violations. Jeremiah also shares with other prophets the concern that Judah turned to other nations, such as Egypt, for military help rather than depending on God for their protection (2:14 – 19).

As mentioned, Jeremiah supported his oral proclamation through symbolic actions. One striking example is found in 13:1 – 11, when God tells the prophet to get a linen loincloth (NIV has "belt," though the modern equivalent would be underwear). God tells him not to wash it, but rather to place it in a cave near the Euphrates River for a period of time and then retrieve it. The dirty underwear is symbolic of the pride that rots away in Judah, destroying the intimate relationship between God and his people.

There are clear indications in these early oracles that Judah rejected Jeremiah's message (8:4 – 12). They not only rejected his message, but persecuted Jeremiah. Jeremiah responded with a series of complaints directed to God, whom he came to blame for putting him in the unwanted position of announcing this bad news (11:18 – 12:6; 15:10 – 11, 15 – 21; 17:14 – 18; 18:19 – 23; 20:7 – 18). The final complaint reveals Jeremiah as a deeply conflicted spokesperson for God. He begins by accusing God of deceiving him (20:7, perhaps in reference to God's promise that he would rescue him [1:8]). He complains that people persecute him for his message. He tries to refrain from speaking, but he cannot help himself and gets in trouble. He then shifts, like a lament psalm, to a statement of confidence in

God (20:11–13), only to end by cursing the day he was born. No wonder Jeremiah has been called "the weeping prophet."

Chapters 25–29 are mostly prose oracles and stories about Jeremiah. They are distinguished from the preceding section of the book in that most of them are dated to years within a specific king's reign. Jeremiah 25:1–14, for instance, is dated to the fourth year of Jehoiakim (605/604 BC) and summarizes many of the themes of the previous chapters, but adds that Judah will spend seventy years in exile. The rest of chapter 25 speaks of the judgment that will come on the nations by saying that they will all drink from God's cup of wrath. Also in the reign of Jehoiakim, Jeremiah was threatened while preaching in the temple area (see also chap. 7; he was a priest as well as a prophet). Chapters 27 and 28 recount an interaction with a false prophet named Hananiah during the reign of Zedekiah, the last king of Judah. While Jeremiah confronted the people by wearing a wooden yoke on his neck, representing their need to submit to Nebuchadnezzar the Babylonian king, he was confronted by Hananiah, who accused Jeremiah of lying and rejected Jeremiah's claim that God would judge Judah, so he proclaimed peace. Later, God told Jeremiah to go back and announce that Hananiah was the one who lied, and because the people listened to him, they would now be put in an iron yoke. The section ends with a letter to the exiles in Babylon and also an exchange with another false prophet, named Shemaiah (chap. 29). The letter is addressed to those who were exiled already in 597 BC (see Authorship and Date below) and tells them to settle into their new location in Babylon because they will be there for a significant period of time. The latter is an oracle against Shemaiah because he plotted to get Jeremiah arrested.

The bulk of Jeremiah's salvation oracles is found in the next major section of the book (chaps. 30–33), though why they are placed here in the collection is not clear, since the book reverts to judgment oracles right afterward. Traditionally, this section is known as the Book of Consolation or Comfort. The first two chapters are written in poetry, and the second two are prose. The message is clear: after judgment God will restore the remnant. Strikingly, God promises to make a new covenant with his people, since they did not live up to the old one (31:31–34)—a new covenant that will be more intimate, more intense, more internal, and more immediate. This passage plays a significant role in the New Testament (see Connections below). Jeremiah continues his use of prophetic sign acts in this section as well, as illustrated by his purchase of his cousin Hanamel's property (chap. 32), indicating that indeed the people of God will eventually return and inhabit the land again.

Jeremiah 34–38 returns to stories about Jeremiah and prose oracles of judgment that are dated to specific kings' reigns (though not themselves in chronological order). Jeremiah 39 then gives an account of the fall of Jerusalem, since the people steadfastly refused to repent.

Jeremiah 40–45 narrates the events that follow the fall of Jerusalem. The Babylonians give Jeremiah the choice whether to go into exile or to stay in the land with those who are left behind. Jeremiah chooses the latter, but intrigues continue. The Babylonians make Judah a province of their vast empire, leaving a garrison of troops and appointing a Jewish governor named Gedaliah, a person who is sympathetic to Jeremiah. However, remnants of the Judean army under a Davidic descendant named Ishmael plot to assassinate the governor and destroy the Babylonian garrison. Ishmael flees the country, leaving the people to face the likely wrath of Nebuchadnezzar. At first the people respond correctly by asking Jeremiah to ask God to guide them, but when Jeremiah announces that God wants them to stay in the land, they reject his message and force him to go with them to Egypt. This narrative reveals that the people have not learned the important lesson that they need to listen to God through his prophet, and Jeremiah tells them that judgment will reach them in Egypt.

The book, though, is not yet done. The final major section (chaps. 46–51) is a series of oracles against the foreign nations (Egypt, Philistia, Moab, Ammon, Edom, Damascus, Kedar, Hazor, Elam, and Babylon). Surprisingly, the book ends with yet another account of the fall of Jerusalem (chap. 52, which is very similar to chap. 39). The final editor of the book likely did not want the readers to end with the triumphant note of the defeat of enemies that had been so cruel to them, so he reminded them of their own sin and judgment.

Authorship and Date: Who Wrote Jeremiah and When?

The superscription (1:1–3) informs the reader that the book contains "the words of Jeremiah son of Hilkiah, one of the priests at Anathoth in the territory of Benjamin." This statement connects Jeremiah with the prophetic oracles that follow, but does not necessarily mean that he wrote every word of the book as it now stands. It is possible, and perhaps even likely, that at least some of the stories about Jeremiah were written by a later disciple—maybe Baruch, who is mentioned as his associate in a number of places in the book (32:12–16; 36; 45).

The superscription also states that Jeremiah ministered from the thirteenth year of King Josiah (626 BC) until the eleventh year of Zedekiah (587 BC). This period of time was turbulent, as we can learn from the historical books of the Old Testament (particularly Kings and Chronicles) as well as from other ancient Near Eastern sources, particularly Babylonian ones.

The year 626 BC is significant not only as the time when God called Jeremiah to minister as a prophet, but also as the year when Nabopolassar proclaimed himself king of Babylon and began a revolt against Assyria, which had dominated the Near East since the second half of the eighth century. Even so, it was not until 612 BC that the Babylonians succeeded in defeating Nineveh, Assyria's capital, and even then the remnants of the Assyrians continued to survive in the region around the city of Haran. In 609 BC the Egyptian pharaoh Neco marched up the coast of Judah to bring his army to support the Assyrians against the Babylonians in order to protect their own interests by keeping a weakened Assyria as a buffer between them and Babylon. Josiah, however, ambushed Neco at Megiddo in support of the Babylonians, since Judah had been an unwilling vassal of Assyria for so long. Josiah died in the effort, and Neco also failed in his attempt to aid the Assyrians, who were at that time totally eradicated. As he retreated to Egypt, Neco manipulated the throne in Jerusalem by removing Josiah's heir, Jehoahaz, from the throne and replacing him with his pro-Egyptian brother, Jehoiakim. In spite of Neco's efforts, Babylon continued to expand down into Syria and Palestine, so in 605 BC King Nebuchadnezzar, Nabopolassar's son and heir, managed to make Jehoiakim submit to him as a vassal (Dan. 1:1–2). However, Jehoiakim, likely hoping for support from Egypt, rebelled against Babylon in 597 BC.

By the time Nebuchadnezzar and his army reached Jerusalem, Jehoiakim had been replaced by his son Jehoiachin, who was quickly subdued and exiled by the Babylonians. Nebuchadnezzar also deported a number of other leading citizens to Babylon, including a young priest named Ezekiel. Thus, in 597 BC Nebuchadnezzar placed Zedekiah, a third son of Josiah, on the throne. Yet even he was looking for the opportunity to revolt against the divinely authorized message of Jeremiah, and he did so in 587 BC. This time Nebuchadnezzar completely subdued Judah, turning it from a vassal state to a province, destroying its public buildings—most devastatingly the temple—and deporting a large number of people.

These events provide the important background to Jeremiah's oracles. Above we already described the historical events connected to the aftermath of the fall of Jerusalem as narrated in chapters 40–45.

Genre: What Style of Literature Is Jeremiah?

As the superscription states in 1:1–3, the book contains the "words" of Jeremiah as the "word of the LORD" came to him. Thus we are not surprised to see that the bulk of the book includes judgment and salvation oracles of various types. But these types do not exhaust the literary components of the book.

First, Jeremiah utilizes both poetic oracles and prose oracles. Poetic oracles are of two kinds: judgment (the majority of chaps. 1–25) and salvation (chaps. 30–31). Prose oracles also include these two kinds, such as judgment in the temple sermon in chapter 7 and salvation in chapter 32. Jeremiah also delivers oracles against the foreign nations in poetic format (chaps. 46–51), as do many other prophets (see Isa. 13–21; Ezek. 25–32; Obadiah). Finally, Jeremiah's complaints (listed above) are also poetic. Other prose genres besides judgment oracles include biographical material written about Jeremiah (see especially chaps. 26–29 and 34–44). The prophetic sign acts are also presented in a prose format.

Connections: How Does Jeremiah Anticipate the Gospel?

The book of Jeremiah made a strong impression on the writers of the New Testament. There are about forty direct quotations of the book in the New Testament, most in Revelation in connection with the destruction of Babylon (e.g., 50:8 in Rev. 18:4; 50:32 in Rev. 18:8; 51:49–50 in Rev. 18:24).

The most striking and important connection between the book of Jeremiah and the gospel is found in the announcement of the new covenant (31:31–34), described above as a covenant that is more intimate, internal, intense, and immediate than the old covenant. Jesus makes it clear that he establishes the new covenant with his disciples during the

Last Supper when he announces, "This cup is the new covenant in my blood, which is poured out for you" (Luke 22:20). The author of Hebrews cites Jeremiah 31:31–34 in Hebrews 8 to also make the point that God through Jesus established the new covenant with his people because the old covenant failed, not because of God, but because of the people.

The message of the New Testament is that Jesus in the new covenant fulfills the old covenants and thus we enjoy a covenantal relationship with God because we are in relationship with him. (See the chapter on Deuteronomy for more on the covenant.) Thus Jesus fulfills the Davidic covenant (2 Sam. 7) because he is the Messiah, the one who sits on the throne forever. He fulfills the Mosaic covenant as the perfect law keeper as well as the one who suffers the penalties of the law on our behalf. He fulfills the Abrahamic covenant because he is the ultimate expression of the promised Seed (Gen. 12:1–3 and Gal. 3:15–28). He fulfills the Adamic-Noahic creation covenant as the second Adam who brings in life and not death (Rom. 5:12–21).

Recommended Resources

Dearman, A. *Jeremiah, Lamentations*. NIVAC. Grand Rapids: Zondervan, 2002.

Fretheim, T. E. *Jeremiah*. Macon, GA: Smyth and Helwys, 2002.

Longman, T. *Jeremiah, Lamentations*. Repackaged ed. UBCS. Grand Rapids: Baker, 2012.

Questions for Reflection and Discussion

1. What is the main message of Jeremiah? Read Jeremiah 7:1–15. How does this passage fit in with this message?
2. What message does Jeremiah have for the foreign nations that have oppressed God's people (see chaps. 46–51 in particular)?
3. What are prophetic sign acts (read Jer. 19:1–20:6 for example), and how do you think they affected the people who observed them?
4. Read Jeremiah 20:7–18. Why did Jeremiah complain to and about God so much? Did he have any justification to do so?
5. What makes the new covenant (31:31–34) new? What is its connection with the New Testament?
6. What is the historical background to the prophecy of Jeremiah? Is this background important to know as one reads Jeremiah today? Why or why not?

chapter twenty-two

THE BOOK OF LAMENTATIONS

Content: What Is Lamentations About?

The book of Lamentations is composed of five poems (one in each chapter). The first four are alphabetic acrostics, and the fifth poem is acrostic-like. An alphabetic acrostic is a poem in which the opening word of each unit begins with a successive letter of the alphabet. The Hebrew alphabet has twenty-two letters, and chapters 1, 2, and 4 have twenty-two verses, one for each letter. Chapter 3 stands out, since it has sixty-six verses, three for every letter. Chapter 5 has twenty-two verses, but is not an acrostic. Because acrostic forms typically communicate wholeness, the switch away from acrostics signifies that resolution between God and Israel has not yet arrived.

The first poem (chap. 1) personifies Jerusalem as a weeping widow; the poet thus attempts to elicit the reader's (and God's) pity for the destruction of that city. Once a queen, she is now deserted by friends and lovers (representing other nations). While trying to elicit compassion, the poet is mindful of the fact that Jerusalem has brought this suffering on itself by its sin (1:8–9, 14, 18).

The second poem describes God coming as a warrior against Jerusalem. While human agents (the Babylonians) destroyed Jerusalem, the poet knows full well the divine reality behind the scenes. It was God who came in his anger to destroy the city. Again, though aware of Jerusalem's guilt, the poet paints a pitiful picture of the survivors of the destruction (2:11–12). God's wrath has come with unprecedented devastation (2:20).

Chapter 3 draws attention to itself by being so much longer than the other poems. It is also the only place in the book that expresses real hope of resolution between God and his people. The poet again uses personification, but this time Jerusalem/Judah is presented as a man—probably a soldier—who is being afflicted by God. This man of affliction suffers deeply, but then also states that God's great love means that "his compassions never fail" (3:22). He thus encourages patience in the midst of suffering. In the last verses of the chapter, the poet calls on God to take vengeance against those who destroyed the city (3:64–66).

Two voices are heard in chapter 4. The narrator speaks in verses 1–16, while we hear the community's voice in the remainder of the chapter. We can detect a kind of sad, exhausted awe at the extent and intensity of the damage to property and especially to people.

The final chapter is a prayer on behalf of the community, asking God to remember and restore it. The community again describes Jerusalem's former glory and present destitution. The people then ask God why he continues to harm them, and the chapter concludes with a final call for restoration.

Authorship and Date: Who Wrote Lamentations and When?

The book does not name an author. Traditionally, Jeremiah is thought to have written the book, but there is no concrete evidence of this. The current view is that the tone of Lamentations, bemoaning the destruction of Jerusalem, is at odds with the tone of Jeremiah in the book of that name, where he comes to see God's judgment as appropriate due to sin. Not only that, but the book of Jeremiah tells us that he was forcibly taken to Egypt soon after the beginning of the exile, and the book of Lamentations has the appearance at least of being written by someone still in the destroyed Jerusalem.

It is highly likely that the book was written soon after the destruction of the city at the hands of the Babylonians. Although some argue, based on analogies with the Sumerian city laments (see Genre below), that the book was actually written as part of a liturgy performed during the rebuilding of the temple, the emotional power of the book fits better with a date of composition close to the actual destruction.

Genre: What Style of Literature Is Lamentations?

The book's genre is also its name; it is a lamentation. A lament is a cry spoken when life falls apart. Laments are well known in the psalms, prayers to God by individuals and communities that have suffered in some way. The book of Lamentations is a city lament, written, as we have seen above, in the aftermath of the destruction of Jerusalem by the Babylonian armies in 586 BC. As a lament, the book gives voice to the pain, suffering, disappointment, and anger of the survivors of the destruction. It also expresses the guilt and hope of the survivors. Through a combination of confession, cajoling, perseverance, cries, and screams, the poet hopes to provoke God to restore them.

Lamentations shares the emotional tone, motifs, literary style, and subject matter with a group of city laments written in Sumerian in the last century of the third millennium BC. These were written in the context of the destruction of the city of Ur and neighboring cities by invaders from the east and the west of lower Mesopotamia. We know of five such compositions by the following names:

> The Lamentation over the Destruction of Ur
> The Lamentation over the Destruction of Sumer and Ur
> The Nippur Lament
> The Eridu Lament
> The Uruk Lament

It could be objected that the time difference is much too great between the biblical book and these Sumerian laments, but there are other city laments known between these times that are written in Akkadian, the language of the Babylonians and Assyrians. What is clear is that the biblical book is writing in a literary tradition that was in use for many centuries.

Connections: How Does Lamentations Anticipate the Gospel?

The book of Lamentations, especially in chapter 3, presents a picture of God as a warrior moving against his sinful people in judgment. Of course, this book is not the only place in the Bible that describes God as a warrior. Most of the time in the Old Testament, God fights on behalf of his people (see the book of Joshua), though on other occasions he does war against his sinful people, as at the battle of Ai (Josh. 7) and during the time of Eli (1 Sam. 4). Yet Lamentations is the most striking example of God's warfare against his people.

That said, the Old Testament does not end on the note of Judah's defeat. The exilic and postexilic prophets have a message of hope that

God the warrior will come in the future to free his people from their oppressors (Dan. 7; Zech. 14; Mal. 4). The fulfillment of this expectation comes with Jesus Christ, who first defeats the spiritual powers and authorities by his victory over them on the cross (Col. 2:13–15) and then finally defeats all evil forces — human and spiritual — at the second coming (Rev. 19:11–21).

Recommended Resources

Dearman, A. *Jeremiah, Lamentations.* NIVAC. Grand Rapids: Zondervan, 2002.

Longman, T. *Jeremiah, Lamentations.* NIBCOT. Peabody, MA: Hendrickson, 2008.

Provan, I. *Lamentations.* NCB. Grand Rapids: Eerdmans, 1992.

Questions for Reflection and Discussion

1. What is an acrostic? Where are acrostics found in Lamentations, and how do they contribute to the book's meaning?
2. How does the author of Lamentations use personification in the book?
3. What connection does the book of Lamentations have to ancient Near Eastern literature?
4. How does Lamentations fit into the theology of the Divine Warrior of the whole Bible?
5. Where is the message of hope found in Lamentations?
6. How does the book end?

chapter twenty-three

THE BOOK
OF EZEKIEL

Content: What Is Ezekiel About?

Ezekiel has one of the clearest structures of the prophetic books. The macrostructure is similar to that found in Isaiah and Zephaniah in that all three books (1) begin with a series of oracles oriented largely to judgment during the historical moment in which the prophet himself lived, then (2) turn to an extended section of oracles against the foreign nations, and (3) conclude with prophecies of blessing more oriented to a distant future.

But even before the judgment oracles that dominate the first part of the book, we hear of Ezekiel's prophetic commissioning in chapters 1–3. Like Isaiah before him (Isa. 6), Ezekiel receives a magnificent vision of the glory of God, though not in the temple, but instead in pagan Babylon. God appears to him on his chariot accompanied by the powerful cherubim. Such a vision of God's glory encourages Ezekiel for his difficult task of prophetic ministry.

The next twenty-one chapters (4–24) contain oracles of judgment against sinful Judah and Jerusalem. These chapters include symbolic actions, such as depicting a devastating siege against Jerusalem on a clay tablet (4:1–3), and verbal oracles, including one announcing the end of the land (chap. 7). Chapters 8–11 narrate the departure of the glory of God from the temple in anticipation of its destruction and due to Judah's sin, especially the sin of idolatry. Ezekiel describes how God rises from his throne in the Holy of Holies to meet the cherubim who accompany his chariot in the courtyard. The final scene pictures God over the mountains to the east of Jerusalem. Oracles that describe the sins of Israel and Jerusalem along with the coming judgment continue in chapters 12–24. This section concludes with a sad note concerning the death of Ezekiel's wife (24:15–27). God commands him not to publicly mourn for her, using her death and Ezekiel's response as a sign of the future when the exiles, already in Babylon since 597 BC (see below), will hear that Jerusalem has been destroyed.

Oracles against the foreign nations follow in chapters 25–32. Many prophets include such oracles (see Isa. 13–23; Jer. 46–51; Amos 1–2; Obadiah; Nahum). Ezekiel's oracles are directed against Ammon, Moab, Edom, Tyre, Egypt, and Lebanon. Most of the oracles are short and charge Israel's immediate neighbors because of their gloating over the destruction of Jerusalem and for their giving aid to their enemies. Tyre, an important trade center and seaport, receives lengthy attention also for its complicity in the fall of Jerusalem. Notable are the extensive allusions to Canaanite mythology—for instance, the depiction of the king's pride by describing him as a select cherub guarding the gate of Edom (18:11–19). Egypt also receives long treatment (chaps. 29–32) because it has had such a horrible influence on Israel as an enemy at times and as an unreliable ally at others.

As mentioned, the long final section of the book (chaps. 33–48) focuses on the blessings that will come on Judah and Jerusalem after the judgment that will purify them. It begins by repeating the prophet's call as a watchman (33:1–20; cf. 3:16–27) and his preaching of individual moral responsibility (33:10–20; cf. chap. 18) and by ending the period of numbness that had followed his wife's death (24:25–27; 33:22). With Jerusalem destroyed, the focus is now on the future city and the people of God.

Many of the prophetic descriptions of the restored people of God that follow are highly enigmatic. Care and caution need to be taken in the proper interpretation of this highly symbolic language. An example includes the description of the restored community found in chapters 40–48, which centers on a future temple (chaps. 40–43)— to which the glory of God returns (43:1–5) after earlier abandoning the temple (chaps. 8–11)—and also a new settlement of the tribes of Israel (47:13–48:29). In the actual return from exile, a temple is rebuilt, but one that does not compare in glory to the first temple, and the twelve tribes are not restored to the full land of Israel.

It would be hard to take the second temple and Israel's restoration to the land as a fulfillment of the glorious vision of Ezekiel. However, it would also be a mistake to insist that the fulfillment must be a literal third temple built within present-day Jerusalem. The temple represents the presence of God, and therefore, rather than its being merely a physical temple, Ezekiel's vision looks forward to a time when God's presence will be in the midst of his people (see below under Connections).

Authorship and Date: Who Wrote Ezekiel and When?

Ezekiel does not have a superscription like many other prophetic books, but it makes it very clear from the start that the prophetic visions and the narratives about the prophet come from Ezekiel himself, who speaks in the first person.

Ezekiel was a priest (1:3) who was thirty years old when he was commissioned as a prophet (1:1). A priest had to be thirty years old to take up priestly service (Num. 4:3), but since he was already in exile by this time and separated from the holy place, Ezekiel was denied that role. But his membership in a priestly family reveals itself throughout the book in Ezekiel's concern with the temple and its rituals.

This priest-prophet was among those who were deported to Babylon when Nebuchadnezzar seized the city in 597 BC after the rebellion of Jehoiakim. By the time the Babylonian king reached Jerusalem, Jehoiakim was off the throne, and his son Jehoiachin was ruling. Nebuchadnezzar quickly subdued the city and carted off to Babylon many leading citizens, including the king and Ezekiel, and turned the crown over to Zedekiah (2 Kings 23:36 – 24:17).

Ezekiel includes a number of chronological notes in the book that allow us to date the action and the oracles with some precision.

Thus Ezekiel's prophecy spans the period 593 to 573. Ezekiel had been taken to Babylon in the deportation of 597, and from Babylon he spoke about the continued sin of the people in Jerusalem. He ministered through the period of the destruction of Jerusalem and the further exile of 586 BC.

Genre: What Style of Literature Is Ezekiel?

The book of Ezekiel is intensely personal. We cannot but enter into the prophet's own experience of awe, fear, distress, revulsion, agony, and other emotions when reading it. One reason for this is that Ezekiel is the only prophetic book written entirely in the first person. We

Reference	Yr/Mon/ Day	Julian calendar	Event
1:1	30/4/5	July 31, 593	Call narrative
1:2	5/4(?)/5	July 31, 593	Call narrative
8:1	6/6/5	Sept. 17, 592	Vision of events in Jerusalem
20:1	7/5/10	Aug. 14. 591	Elders come to inquire
24:1	9/10/10	Jan. 15, 588	Siege of Jerusalem begins
26:1	11/-/1	Between Apr. 587 and Apr. 586	Oracle against Tyre
29:1	10/10/12	Jan. 7, 587	Oracle against Egypt
29:17	27/1/1	Apr. 26, 587	Egypt instead of Tyre
30:20	11/1/7	Apr. 29, 587	Oracle against Pharaoh
31:1	11/3/1	June 21, 587	Oracle against Pharaoh
32:1	12/12/1	Mar. 3, 585	Oracle against Pharaoh
32:17	12/-/15	Between Apr. 586 and Apr. 585	Oracle against Egypt
33:21	12/10/5	Jan. 8, 585	Escapee from Jerusalem armies
40:1	25/1/10	Apr. 28, 573	Vision of restored Jerusalem

encounter Ezekiel's experiences, not through a third-person narrative, but as he describes them from his own mouth.

A wide variety of literary forms are used in the book. There are funeral laments (19; 27; 28:11 – 19; 32:2 – 16); fables and allegories (15; 16; 17; 23); visions (1:1 – 3:15; 8 – 11; 37:1 – 14; 40 – 48); symbolic actions (4:1 – 5:17; 12:1 – 20; 21:11 – 29; 24:1 – 27; 33:21 – 22; 37:15 – 28); historico-theological narrative (20); legal sayings (14:1 – 11; 18; 22:1 – 16); ritual and priestly regulations (43:18 – 27; 44:17 – 31; 45:18 – 46:12); disputation oracles (33:1 – 20); and many shorter forms, such as quotations, oaths, sayings, and proverbs. The prophet enlisted a panoply of literary genres effectively.

Connections: How Does Ezekiel Anticipate the Gospel?

Ezekiel's contribution to the theology of the New Testament is rich and varied and unable to be fully captured here. The New Testament directly or indirectly cites the book some sixty-five times, most citations being found in the book of Revelation. Only a few examples can be given here.

Ezekiel 34 castigates the failed shepherds (rulers) of Israel and Judah. They do not take care of the sheep. God himself will care for the sheep. He promises to "place over them one shepherd, my servant David, and he will tend them; he will tend them and be their shepherd" (34:23). The New Testament understands Jesus, David's descendant and the Messiah, to be the good shepherd (John 10).

Ezekiel had a vision of a river trickling from south of the altar and turning into a great torrent that brought life everywhere it went and turned the Dead Sea into fresh water (47:1–12). Jesus identified himself as the source of this life-giving water when he spoke with a woman at a well in Samaria (John 4:10–14). Ezekiel's vision also stands behind the picture of the river of life that flows from the throne of God in the New Jerusalem (Rev. 22:1).

A final example concerns the future temple envisioned by Ezekiel in chapters 40–43. We commented earlier that this vision neither was fulfilled in the building of the second temple in the immediate postexilic period nor would be fulfilled in the literal building of a third temple in Jerusalem. Rather, this vision is fulfilled in the coming of Jesus Christ, who is the very presence of God. John speaks of Jesus as the Word, who "became flesh and made his dwelling among us. We have seen his glory, the glory of the one and only Son, who came from the Father, full of grace and truth" (John 1:14). The author of Hebrews describes Jesus as "the radiance of God's glory and the exact representation of his being" (Heb. 1:3). In the New Jerusalem there will be no temple "because the Lord God Almighty and the Lamb are its temple" (Rev. 21:22). Jesus himself is the fulfillment of Ezekiel's expectation.

Recommended Resources

Duguid, I. *Ezekiel*. NIVAC. Grand Rapids: Zondervan, 1999.

Longman, T. "The Glory of God in the Old Testament." Pages 47–48 in *The Glory of God*. Edited by C. W. Morgan and R. A. Peterson. Wheaton, IL: Crossway, 2010.

Questions for Reflection and Discussion

1. How does God's glory figure in Ezekiel's prophecy?
2. What can we say about the structure of the book of Ezekiel?

3. What is the significance of the picture of the future temple in Ezekiel 40–43?
4. Who was Ezekiel, and where did he minister?
5. Describe the time period during which Ezekiel prophesied.

chapter twenty-four

THE BOOK OF DANIEL

Content: What Is Daniel About?

The book of Daniel contains two main parts. The first six chapters narrate six stories of Daniel in a foreign court. The second six chapters present four apocalyptic visions (see below). Daniel is also written in two languages, Hebrew and Aramaic, though the language split does not exactly conform to the division between stories and visions. That is, 1:1–2:4 and chaps. 8–12 are in Hebrew, while 2:5–7:28 is in Aramaic. No one has persuasively explained why the book is written in two languages.

In spite of this variety of genre and language, the book has one central overarching theme communicated by all the stories and the visions: In spite of present difficulties, God is in control, and he will have the victory.

This theme is critically important to the historical period of the setting of the book as well as throughout time. Daniel 1:1–2 reveals that the action of the book begins when Nebuchadnezzar of Babylon reduced King Jehoiakim of Jerusalem to vassal status (605 BC), symbolized by turning over some of the utensils of the temple as well as political hostages—namely, four young men from noble families: Daniel, Azariah, Hananiah, and Mishael.

To illustrate how the main theme works in the book, we will look at chapters 1, 2, and 7.

Daniel 1 describes how Nebuchadnezzar attempts to "Babylonianize" Daniel and his three friends by subjecting them to an education that has the purpose to "teach them the language and literature of the Babylonians" (1:4). This curriculum includes many elements that prove to be toxic to the religion of Daniel and his friends, including divinatory practices such as dream interpretation. Nebuchadnezzar also prescribes a food regimen for them with the purpose of making them look like the Babylonian wise men we know from ancient art, round-faced and slightly chubby.

The four Judean men, however, refuse to follow the Babylonian diet of rich meat and wine that would surely have produced the desired look. They refuse it, not because the food is ritually unclean or indicates political allegiance or is food offered to idols, but rather because they want to allow God room to work. At the end of the chapter, when the four are recognized as the best in their class, Nebuchadnezzar thinks that their wisdom and physical look are the result of his education and diet, but Daniel and the three friends (as well as all who read the story) know that it is God who makes them look so healthy in spite of their meager diet of vegetables and water.

In chapter 2 we learn that God, not Nebuchadnezzar's education, gives them true wisdom. As mentioned, they learn dream interpretation according to the Babylonian system in their school. The dreamer tells the interpreter the content of his dream, and then the interpreter goes and consults the dream-interpretation books. It is no surprise that the wise men of Babylon are shocked when Nebuchadnezzar demands that they first tell him what he dreamed. No king has ever asked anything like this before (2:10–11). They cannot interpret without knowing the dream. Nebuchadnezzar thus determines to kill all the wise men because they have failed to interpret his dream. However, when the executioner comes to Daniel and the three friends, they ask for time to pray. In response, God reveals both the content of the dream and its interpretation. The interpretation is very similar to the message of the apocalyptic vision in chapter 7, which we will examine next.

Chapters 1 and 2 (as well as the stories in chaps. 3–6) illustrate well that in spite of present difficulties, God is in control and will have the victory. Not only can God's people survive in captivity, but they can even thrive as Daniel and the three friends are promoted higher and higher in the Babylonian hierarchy.

Chapter 7 well illustrates the purpose and function of the four apocalyptic visions (chaps. 7, 8, 9, 10–12). The chapter opens with a description of a vision that comes to Daniel (vv. 1–14). Daniel is disturbed by the vision but does not understand it until an interpreting angel comes to him. The vision consists of four beasts arising consecutively out of a chaotic sea. The sea itself is a symbol of disorder and evil, and these beasts are associated with it. The first beast is a hybrid having characteristics of a lion, an eagle, and a human being. Such hybrids were considered terrifying to the Israelites. The second beast is a bear rending its prey, and the third another hybrid, this time part leopard and part bird, having four heads and four wings. The vision climaxes with the fourth animal, which is not even organic. It has iron teeth (v. 7) and bronze claws (v. 19). It also has ten horns, representing great power, and the focus is on one of those horns, a little one that speaks boastfully.

Interpretations differ as to the exact identity of these beasts and the horns. What is clear is that the beasts represent evil human kingdoms that oppress the people of God (v. 17). That is really all that is important to know. These kingdoms seem to have their way with the people of God, but the reality is revealed in the second part of the vision (vv. 9–14). There the Ancient of Days, a clear representation of God, takes his seat to render judgment. Into his presence comes one like the son of man riding a cloud (vv. 13–14). In the Old Testament, "son of man" is a phrase describing a human being, but the one who rides a cloud is always God (Pss. 18:9; 68:4; 104:3; Isa. 19:1; Nah. 1:3). The New Testament connects the son of man with Jesus Christ (see below). The end of the vision depicts the son of man leading the saints of the Most High and destroying the beasts and establishing an "everlasting kingdom" (7:27). Once again, readers learn that in spite of present difficulties (when it looks as if evil human kingdoms are in control), God is in control and will have the final victory.

Authorship and Date: Who Wrote Daniel and When?

No author or date is explicitly given for the writing of the book of Daniel. The burning issue surrounding the book has to do with whether or not the visions and interpretations of chapters 7–12 actually come from the sixth century BC, the time during which the book situates Daniel (through the neo-Babylonian period into the first years of the Persian period; 605–537 BC). The first six chapters are narratives written about Daniel, and the prophecies themselves are set within a narrative framework that could have been written after the sixth century, but the question of when the visions occurred is the real debated issue.

The book itself places the visions in specific times in the sixth century (chap. 7, the first year of Belshazzar; chap. 8, the third year of Belshazzar; chap. 9, the first year of Darius; chaps. 10–12, the third year of Cyrus). The visions speak of events in the subsequent centuries as future events; in other words, the visions are prophetic.

However, some scholars—even among those who believe that prophecy is possible—have difficulty believing that these are actual prophecies, but rather are prophecies "after the fact." The problem for these scholars is that the predictions are so specific and so correct as to future events that it seems as if it is more like prophecy being written in the light of the events. In addition, the final vision describes the events of the third through the mid-second centuries very accurately until the end, when the prediction of the final king (usually identified as Antiochus Epiphanes IV) mischaracterizes his death (11:40–45). To many scholars, therefore, it appears that the only real attempt at prophecy fails. Thus the conclusion is that the visions were written in the mid-second century BC, and many scholars further conclude that that is the date of the book as a whole.

On occasion, the attempt is made to soften the idea that this would be deception or misrepresentation by observing that the ancient world knew various genres of literature (such as Akkadian literary prophecies and intertestamental Jewish apocalypses) that would signal to the original audience what was going on. The problem with this approach is that these extrabiblical texts themselves worked on deception.

Those who advocate a sixth-century date for the visions interpret 11:40–45 as referring to the end of time rather than to Antiochus Epiphanes. This debate will continue.

Genre: What Style of Literature Is Daniel?

Daniel uses two major genres. In chapters 1–6 there are six stories of Daniel in a foreign court. They are appropriately described as theological history (see the chapters on Genesis and Kings). More specifically they might be called "court tales," because they focus on the main characters, Daniel and his three friends, in the Babylonian and then the Persian courts. These six stories serve an important didactic purpose for people who live during periods of similar oppression by hostile powers. They give encouragement to people of God that not only can they survive oppression and persecution, but they can even thrive.

Chapters 7 – 12 contain four apocalyptic visions — the only undisputed apocalypses in the Old Testament. While apocalyptic and prophecy share many features, including an interest in the future, there are also critical differences. In the first place, there is a difference in the mode and purpose of divine revelation. Prophets receive a direct word from God and communicate it to the people with the hope that they will repent and avert the coming divine judgment. By contrast, God never speaks to Daniel. Rather, Daniel has visions, and in response to his bewilderment, an angel comes and interprets the visions' significance. The angel then tells him to keep the meaning secret; there certainly is not encouragement to spread the message broadly. This difference has to do with the purpose of apocalyptic, which is not to elicit repentance from God's people, but to announce the destruction of their persecutors in order to bring comfort to God's people in the midst of their suffering.

This purpose is served by looking — not at the near future, which is the burden of prophets — but beyond to the end of time, when God the warrior will intrude into the historical process and save his people. Apocalyptic is also characterized by an intense use of imagery often drawn from mythological sources — for instance, God's battle against the sea and its monsters (7:1 – 12) and the picture of a divine figure riding on a cloud (7:13 – 14).

Connections: How Does Daniel Anticipate the Gospel?

Daniel provides tremendous inspiration for New Testament reflections on the end of time, when Christ will return. After all, the gist of many of Daniel's visions, serving the theme that God will have victory at the end, is that evil human powers may hold the upper hand now, but the day is coming when God, the warrior, will come and save his people by vanquishing those powers. John the Baptist thought that these prophecies were coming to fulfillment with what we recognize as the first coming of Christ (Matt. 3:7 – 12; 11:2), but Jesus came to war against the spiritual powers and authorities. The New Testament, often using language from the book of Daniel (especially 7:13 – 14; see Matt. 24:30; Mark 13:26; Luke 21:27; Rev. 1:13), sees Jesus as the one who will come and complete God's judgment against evil, both human and spiritual.

Recommended Resources

Goldingay, J. E. *Daniel*. WBC. Nashville: Word, 1989.

Longman, T. *Daniel*. NIVAC. Grand Rapids: Zondervan, 1999.

Lucas, E. *Daniel*. Apollos. Downers Grove, IL: InterVarsity Press, 2002.

Schwab, G. M. *Hope in the Midst of a Hostile World: The Gospel according to Daniel*. Phillipsburg, NJ: P and R Publishing, 2006.

Questions for Review and Discussion

1. What is the theme of Daniel?
2. How does Daniel 3 illustrate the theme? How does Daniel 8?
3. What are the issues surrounding the date of Daniel's composition?
4. Describe apocalyptic literature. What purpose does it serve?

chapter twenty-five

THE BOOK
OF HOSEA

Content: What Is Hosea About?

The book of Hosea is a prophecy that announces judgment on Israel
and, on occasion, on Judah. Beyond the judgment, it envisions a restoration of the relationship between God and his people.

The book roughly falls into two unequal parts. Chapters 1 – 3 use
the marriage metaphor to talk about the trouble between God and
Israel — that is, the concept that God's relationship with Israel is like
that of a husband and wife. In Hosea, like elsewhere (see, for instance,
Ezek. 16 and 23), Israel, the wife, has sinned against her husband and
slept with other men. The book, therefore, opens with God's command to the prophet to go and marry Gomer, a promiscuous woman.

Debate rages as to whether Hosea was actually to marry such
a woman or whether this language is purely symbolic. There is no
reason to reject the idea that God actually had him marry her. (There
is no law, for instance, that prohibits a non-priest from marrying a
prostitute.) Some believe that Gomer was not an ordinary prostitute, but a shrine prostitute, but there is no indication of this. Others
believe that she was spiritually promiscuous, not literally promiscuous, but does it solve the problem to say that God wants him to marry
a woman who breaks the first two commandments rather than the
seventh? What is clear is that this marriage reflects Israel's dysfunctional relationship with God. The three children of this marriage also
indicate that the divine-human relationship has been broken. Their
daughter is named Lo-Ruhamah ("not loved") and their second son
Lo-Ammi ("not my people"). The first son's name is Jezreel, after the
place where Jehu committed murders, for which now he will be pun-

ished by having his dynasty come to an end. (See 2 Kings 9:14 – 29; Jehu was commanded by God to put an end to Ahab's dynasty, but may have overstepped his bounds by killing Ahaziah of Judah.) In a pattern that is repeated throughout the book, this judgment will be followed by restoration (1:10 – 2:1).

Chapter 2 reverts to a judgment oracle against Israel, depicted again as the mother (2:2 – 13), followed by a salvation oracle of the restoration of the relationship (2:14 – 23). The brief chapter 3 contains God's command to the prophet to go back to his wife — presumably Gomer — and love her again.

While the first part of Hosea centers on the marriage metaphor, the second part (chaps. 4 – 14) bombards the reader with a series of different images, though with the same overarching message: God will judge his people, but then he will restore them. Rather than a jealous husband, God is pictured as a frustrated shepherd (4:16), a destructive moth or undesired rot (5:12), a ferocious lion (5:14; cf. also 13:7 – 8), and a trapper (7:12). Supporting the theme of salvation, rather than a forgiving husband, God is a healing physician (6:1 – 2), the revivifying rains (6:3), a loving parent (11:3 – 4), a protecting lion (11:10 – 11), a life-giving dew (14:5), and a fertile pine tree (14:8).

Beside images of God, Hosea describes unfaithful Israel and, on occasion, unfaithful Judah as rapidly disappearing morning mist (6:5), hot ovens (7:4 – 7), a silly dove (7:11), a faulty bow (7:16), and a wild donkey (8:9). God's coming judgment upon Israel is likened to harvesting the whirlwind (8:7), the washing away of debris (10:7), and the yoking of a recalcitrant heifer (10:11).

These images communicate Hosea's message even though we find it difficult to delineate a clear structure in chapters 4 – 14. That said, in broad outlines we can break these chapters into two cycles of alternating judgment and salvation. Judgment oracles are found in 4:1 – 10:15, followed by a salvation oracle in 11:1 – 11. Then, in 11:12 – 13:16 we have another series of judgment oracles, followed by a statement concerning Israel's repentance and blessing (14:1 – 8). The book ends with a wisdom admonition to listen and understand and stay on the right path (14:9).

Authorship and Date: Who Wrote Hosea and When?

The superscription of the book (1:1) names the author as Hosea son of Beeri. We know nothing of Hosea apart from this book. He received and imparted God's oracles during the reign of Jeroboam II in the north and the reigns of Uzziah, Jotham, Ahaz, and Hezekiah in the south. Jeroboam was the first of these kings to begin to rule, in 793; Uzziah assumed the throne of Judah in 791. Hezekiah, the last king in the list, ended his reign in 687/6. Of course, this is an impossibly long period of time, and the earliest and latest periods do not seem reflected in the prophecy. Thus Hosea probably began to minister late in Jeroboam's reign (which ended sometime between 753 and 746 BC) and ended his ministry toward the beginning of Hezekiah's rule (perhaps around 715 BC). Hosea is therefore one of the earliest prophets (along with Amos, Micah, and Isaiah).

Genre: What Style of Literature Is Hosea?

Hosea's superscription names the contents of the book "the word of the LORD" (1:1), a way of referring to a collection of prophetic oracles. The book is written predominantly in poetry, although there are two prose oracles (1:2–2:1; 3:1–5). Hosea offers both judgment and salvation oracles. Often it is difficult to delineate the individual oracles in chapters 4–14.

Connections: How Does Hosea Anticipate the Gospel?

The central metaphor of the first three chapters, God's marriage to Israel, is pervasive throughout Scripture. In the Old Testament it is typically used in the negative sense as in Hosea—that is, it is a tarnished relationship, since Israel, the bride, has gone after other lovers. The New Testament appropriates this metaphor from the Old Testament and relates it to the relationship between Christ and the church. Ephesians 5:21–33 speaks of Christ as the husband and the Christian as the bride. Husbands should love their wives as Christ loves the church, and the church should submit to their Christ as wives submit to their husbands. Revelation 19:6–8 speaks of the consummation of all things as a wedding between Christ and the church.

In addition, there are a few, but highly significant quotations from Hosea in the New Testament. Paul (Rom. 9:25) and Peter (1 Peter 2:10; cf. Hos. 1:6, 9; 2:1, 23) both cite the negative-to-positive use of the prophet's children's names to support their contention that the Gentiles are now a part of the people of God. Hosea's sarcastic call to personified Death—"Where, O death, are your plagues? Where, O grave, is your destruction?" (13:14; perhaps reflecting the Canaanite god Mot)—is cited by Paul when he celebrates Christ's victory over death (1 Cor. 15:55). Lastly, and most difficult, is the quotation of Hosea 11:1 ("When Israel was a child, I loved him, and out of Egypt I called my son") in Matthew 2:15 as a prophecy of the return of Jesus from his short sojourn in Egypt.

Recommended Resources

Barrett, M. P. *Love Divine and Unfailing: The Gospel according to Hosea.* Phillipsburg, NJ: P and R Publishing, 2008.

Hubbard, D. A. *Hosea.* TOTC. Downers Grove, IL: InterVarsity Press, 1989.

McComiskey, T. E. "Hosea." Pages 1–237 in *The Minor Prophets: An Exegetical and Expository Commentary.* Edited by T. E. McComiskey. Grand Rapids: Baker, 2009.

Ortlund, Jr., R. C. *Whoredom: God's Unfaithful Wife in Biblical Theology.* Grand Rapids: Eerdmans, 1996.

Questions for Review and Discussion

1. How does Hosea use the marriage metaphor? What makes it particularly appropriate for his message?
2. What is the significance of the names of Hosea's children?
3. Name as many images of God that you can find in chapters 4–14, and describe in your own words what they are saying about God.
4. Name as many images of God's people that you can find in chapters 4–14, and describe in your own words what they are saying about them.
5. How does the New Testament use the prophecy of Hosea in its presentation of the gospel?

chapter twenty-six

THE BOOK OF JOEL

Content: What Is Joel About?

After the superscription (1:1), the book of Joel begins with a verbal depiction of a locust plague and its terrifying consequences and the frightened response of the people (1:2–20). Nothing like this has ever happened before (1:1). All the crops are destroyed and the farmers mourn; all the grapes are eaten, and drunkards wail. The prophet calls people to ritual action; they need to don sackcloth and weep at the altar and keep a fast (1:13–14). The "Day of the LORD" is approaching (1:15) and the food is gone; the prophet leads in a prayer for help (1:16–20).

In chapter 2, Joel announces that the Day of the Lord has come, and he warns of an attack (vv. 1–2). The attack is described in language that makes it difficult to know whether the prophet refers to a second locust plague, where the insects are described like a human army, or whether the attack is by a human army that is depicted as a locust horde (2:3–11). Whichever it is, locust or human, God leads the attack against the people (2:11), and it, too, will result in horrible devastation. In the light of impending doom, the prophet charges the people to repent with the hope of restoring relationship with God and avoiding calamity. This repentance cannot be superficial, but must be sincere—a rending of the heart, not of clothes (2:13). Again, the prophet calls on God's people to fast and to pray at the temple (2:15–17).

In response to the threat, God will remove the locusts so that there will be a healing of the land and the production of crops again (2:18–27). In response to the impending disaster of the Day of the Lord, God will provide salvation for his people. He will pour out his Spirit on all people and will save those who call on his name

(2:28–32). He will also judge the nations (3:1–17). The book ends, however, not on a note of judgment, but with the statement that God's people will experience great blessing (3:18–21).

Authorship and Date: Who Wrote Joel and When?

The book is written by Joel, the son of Pethuel, and although other people by this name are known in the Old Testament, none can be confidently identified with the prophet. Unlike other superscriptions, Joel's does not name contemporary kings, thus making the dating of the book difficult and a matter of educated guesswork based on internal considerations. Thus it is not surprising that scholars have offered dates ranging from the ninth century to the second century BC. One feature of the book that appears relevant and relatively secure is the assumption of a functioning temple (1:9, 13–16; 2:15–17), which would mean that an exilic date is unlikely. The lack of reference to a king and the mention of elders and priests (1:2, 13; 2:16) point more to a second temple rather than a first temple period (post–515 BC). Unfortunately, the naming of nations outside of Israel in the book seems more like a listing of traditional enemies, but the absence of the Assyrians and Babylonians also would point to a postexilic period when the Persians have supplanted the Babylonians who had supplanted the Assyrians. In the final analysis, while we cannot be certain, the most likely date seems in the late sixth or early fifth century BC. One reason the historical echoes are weak may be seen in its identification as a ritual text.

Genre: What Style of Literature Is Joel?

As noted above, the book resists definite dating. The vague historical references likely occur because the book of Joel functioned as a temple liturgy. When military or natural disaster occurred, Joel could serve as a template for corporate lament. Thus, rather than addressing a specific historical event, the book could be reused over the generations. The less specific a text is, the more flexible it is for multiple use.

Connections: How Does Joel Anticipate the Gospel?

The book of Joel is best known to New Testament readers for the latter's use of Joel 2:28–32, which speaks of the future outpouring of

God's Spirit on his people. Joel envisions a day when God will answer Moses' prayer that God will pour his Spirit on all people so that they might be prophets (Num. 11:29). According to Joel's vision, God's Spirit will come on the young as well as the old, women as well as men, not only on free citizens, but also on their servants. The New Testament makes it clear as well that the Spirit comes not only on Jewish people, but also on Gentiles (see Rom. 10:12–13, citing Joel 2:32). The same Spirit who empowered the Old Testament prophets would strengthen the church in its witness to the world (Acts 1:8). Most dramatically, the outpouring of the Spirit on the church occurs on the Day of Pentecost, reversing the effects of the confusion of languages at the time of the Tower of Babel, allowing for the diffusion of the gospel (Acts 2:14–17).

Recommended Resource

Dillard, R. B. "Joel." Pages 239–314 in *The Minor Prophets: An Exegetical and Expository Commentary*. Edited by T. E. McComiskey. Grand Rapids: Baker, 2009.

Questions for Review and Discussion

1. What roles do locusts play in Joel's prophetic oracles?
2. How is the date of the book's composition determined? How confident can we be of this date?
3. Read Joel 2:28–32. What does the passage anticipate? How does the New Testament understand it to be fulfilled?

chapter twenty-seven

THE BOOK OF AMOS

Content: What Is Amos About?

The book of Amos contains three parts. It begins with oracles against the nations (chaps. 1–2), followed by judgment speeches against Israel (chaps. 3–6), and it concludes with reports of prophetic visions (chaps. 7–9).

The oracles charge various nations with sin — specifically, the Gentile nations (Damascus, Gaza, Edom, Ammon, and Moab) with war crimes. One can imagine an Israelite reader enjoying the litany of accusations and savoring the punishment that was coming for those countries. However, the list of charges goes on to include Judah and climaxes with Israel, the northern kingdom being the ultimate target of the prophet's concern. While the accusations against the Gentiles are likely based on either international law or natural law, Judah and Israel have broken God's holy law. In spite of God's care toward them (2:10–11), Israel has sinned, in particular by taking advantage of the vulnerable of society. For their social injustice, both Judah and Israel deserve and will receive God's judgment.

The second part of Amos contains many different types of judgment speeches directed toward Israel. Chapter 3 reflects the prophetic lawsuit form. The plaintiff (God) in this legal accusation and the defendant (Israel) are introduced (3:1a), followed by a short history of the past relationship and the nature of the breach in that relationship (3:1b–2). Verses 3–6 present a series of rhetorical questions that serve as the cross-examination of the defendant. The authority of the prophetic messenger (which is that of a lawyer of the covenant representing God's concerns) is affirmed in verses 7–8.

The surrounding nations serve as witnesses to this legal case (v. 9), and the judgment is announced (vv. 10–15). The rest of this section includes judgment speeches (4:1–13; 5:1–17) and woe oracles (5:18–27; 6:1–14).

In the last three chapters the prophet gives an autobiographical account of the five visions he received. The first four (7:1–3, 4–6, 7–9; 8:1–3) are similar and related to one another, but distinct from the fifth (9:1–10). The first two portray events (locust plague and drought), while the next two present objects (plumb line and fruit basket). In the first pair, Amos intercedes and successfully convinces God to refrain from judgment. In the second pair, the portent of the vision cannot be evaded. Perhaps the first two were delivered early in the prophet's ministry when there was still hope, and the second two after the possibility of repentance was definitively rejected. The rejection of the prophet may be seen in 7:10–17, when Amos is confronted by Amaziah, the false priest at the golden calf shrine at Bethel. In the last vision (9:1–10) the object seen is the Lord himself, and there is no dialogue between God and the prophet; no particular action is mentioned, and the prophet remains a silent listener to the words of God. The book ends with an abrupt shift to a salvation oracle that sees an ultimate restoration. The nations will be rebuilt (9:11–12), and the land of Israel will again be fruitful (9:13–15).

Authorship and Date: Who Wrote Amos and When?

The superscription (1:1) identifies the author of the book as Amos from Tekoa. Tekoa, five miles from Bethlehem, is in the southern kingdom, which is notable, since Amos's prophetic message was delivered in and against the northern kingdom.

In addition, Amos is said to be a shepherd and, in 7:14, one who tends sycamore-fig trees. At face value, this description places him, in socioeconomic terms, in the lower classes. However, some argue that the term that designates him as a shepherd (*noqed*) differentiates him from those who actually tend the flocks (*ro'eh*). An Ugaritic cognate indicates that he might have been a large-scale breeder or broker of herds. An Akkadian word that is related to *noqed* refers to a mid-level manager of a Mesopotamian temple. This information leads some to believe Amos was in charge of the Jerusalem temple's flocks. While this view is possible, we should note that 7:15 explicitly says that he "tends flocks." The fact that he also tended sycamore-fig trees—which some scholars want to excise as a later addition to the manuscript—adds support to the idea that Amos was a lowly, not a wealthy, shepherd.

While the book contains oracles from God that Amos delivered, he seems to deny that he is a prophet: "I was neither a prophet nor the son of a prophet" (7:14). He states this to the false priest, Amaziah, who tells him to take his prophecies back south from where he came. Since both Amaziah and Amos refer to Amos's speech as an act of prophesying (the verbal form of the noun "prophet," *nabi'*), it makes it difficult to determine exactly what Amos is saying. However, the best answer appears to be that Amos denies being a "full-time" or professional prophet. Rather, it appears that God called him to give this particular prophecy and no more.

This view is supported by the date given for his prophetic word in the superscription (1:1). The date is not a range of years, but rather a discrete time: two years before the earthquake that happened during the reigns of Jeroboam II in Israel (784–748 BC) and Uzziah in Judah (769–733 BC). The earthquake, also mentioned in Zechariah 14:5, is of uncertain exact date. We do know that the reigns of Jeroboam and Uzziah were times of unprecedented prosperity, against which Amos will speak. As a consequence of military successes and territorial expansion (2 Kings 14:25–28; 2 Chron. 26:6–8), great wealth accrued to the two kingdoms. However, in spite of this success, Assyrian power was building, providing the background to Amos's warning of a threatened invasion (3:11; 5:3; 6:7–14; 7:9, 17; 9:4).

Genre: What Style of Literature Is Amos?

Amos is a prophetic book. It contains oracles against the nations (see Obadiah), as well as both judgment speeches and salvation oracles that announced future punishment and restoration respectively. These oracles come in a variety of forms. Chapter 3 has the form of a prophetic lawsuit. In addition, the book includes woe oracles (5:18–27; 6:1–4) that are modeled on funeral dirges and announce that Israel was as good as dead. Chapter 7 contains a prophetic lawsuit, and chapters 7 (vv. 1–3, 4–6, 7–9) and 8 (vv. 1–3) present visions in which God shows Amos something, then explains its prophetic significance.

Connections: How Does Amos Anticipate the Gospel?

The New Testament shares Amos's concern with social justice and the abuse of the poor (see 1 Cor. 11:22; James 2:1 – 10). Christians should care for the needy, not exploit them (James 1:27; 5:1 – 6). God cares for the poor (James 2:5).

Amos is specifically cited in several New Testament passages. Paul's exhortation to "hate evil and cling to what is good" may have been drawn from Amos (5:15; Rom. 12:9). Stephen cites the prophet to recall Israel's national idolatry during the wilderness wandering (5:25; Acts 7:42). Perhaps of greatest interest is the citation of Amos 9:11 – 12 in Acts 15:16 – 17. Although the source for the actual text cited in Acts is difficult to establish, at the council of Jerusalem James appears to argue that the incorporation of the Gentiles into the church fulfills God's promise to reunify Israel. Rebuilding David's fallen tent and repairing its breaches (the breakup of the united kingdom) does not apply to the physical nation of Israel alone; it includes the ingathering of the nations.

Recommended Resources

Hubbard, D. A. *Joel and Amos.* TOTC. Downers Grove, IL: InterVarsity Press, 1989.

Niehaus, J. "Amos." Pages 315 – 494 in *The Minor Prophets: An Exegetical and Expository Commentary.* Edited by T. E. McComiskey. Grand Rapids: Baker, 2009.

Ryken, L. "Amos." Pages 337 – 47 in *The Complete Literary Guide to the Bible.* Edited by L. Ryken and T. Longman. Grand Rapids: Zondervan, 1993.

Questions for Review and Discussion

1. How does Amos use the oracles against the foreign nations in its condemnation of Judah and Israel?
2. Who was Amos?
3. Why does Amos dispute the claim that he was a prophet?
4. Describe the time period in which Amos prophesied.
5. What use does the New Testament make of Amos?

chapter twenty-eight

THE BOOK
OF OBADIAH

Content: What Is Obadiah About?

Obadiah, the shortest book in the Old Testament, is an oracle against Edom that announces its future destruction. Edom was located to the south and east of the Dead Sea, from the Wadi Zered to the Gulf of Aqaba. It was the site of important trade and therefore grew wealthy. It was also known for its wisdom.

The Bible records a long history of frequent contact between Israel and Edom. The Edomites are descendants of Esau (Gen. 36:1–9), the brother of Jacob/Israel. Thus the prophet refers to the Edomites as close relatives (vv. 10, 12).

The prophet begins by announcing that Edom will experience complete destruction (vv. 2–9); not one grape will be left in its vineyard (v. 5). Its former allies will turn against it to destroy it.

The next section presents the reasons why Edom will be singled out (vv. 10–14). The Edomites celebrated when Israel was attacked by another nation and exiled. They took advantage of Israel's weakness and killed many of its citizens and incorporated some of its territory. After all, Israel, as we commented above, was Edom's "brother" (v. 12).

The final section again envisions the destruction of Edom, but adds that Israel will be restored (vv. 15–21). What Edom did to Israel will now come on Edom. Then the territory will be restored to Israel.

Authorship and Date: Who Wrote Obadiah and When?

The superscription names Obadiah as the author (1:1), but this Obadiah cannot be identified with any of the other Obadiahs mentioned in the Hebrew Bible. However, the superscription does not give the time period for the prophecy, so we are dependent on internal considerations. As mentioned above, the prophecy states that Edom was guilty of crimes against Israel and for this reason would be punished in the future. It also indicates that Edom perpetrated its crimes at a time when Israel had been weakened by another nation that exiled some of its citizens. The most likely period, then, is the time right after the destruction of Jerusalem by the Babylonians in 586 BC. This viewpoint is supported by references to Edom's evil actions toward God's people in Psalm 137:7 and Lamentations 4:21–22.

Genre: What Style of Literature Is Obadiah?

Obadiah is an oracle against a foreign nation. From the beginning of the prophetic movement, prophets spoke not only against Israel, but also against other countries. Moses confronted the Pharaoh of Egypt (Ex. 3:10). Jeremiah was called to be "a prophet to the nations" (Jer. 1:5). All the prophets, with the exception of Hosea and Haggai, contain such oracles. The largest collections are found in Isaiah 13–23; Jeremiah 46–51; Ezekiel 25–32, 35; and Amos 1–2.

Edom is the subject of more separate oracles against foreign nations than any other nation. There are other oracles against Edom in Isaiah 34:5–15; Jeremiah 49:7–22; Ezekiel 25:12–14; 35; Amos 1:11–12; and Malachi 1:2–5. However, Obadiah is distinctive in that it is completely an oracle against that single foreign nation. Verses 1–9 have many close verbal and thematic links to Jeremiah 49:7–16, but the direction of the dependence is not clear.

Oracles against the foreign nations like Obadiah have consistent theological underpinnings. First, they express the universal rule of Yahweh. God is not just the God of Israel, but also the God of the nations. Second, the oracles reflect the theology of the Abrahamic covenant that God will "bless those who bless you, and whoever curses you I will curse" (Gen. 12:3). Edom has hurt Israel, and now the favor will be returned.

Connections: How Does Obadiah Anticipate the Gospel?

The conflict between Jacob and Esau, between Israel and Edom, has its echoes in the New Testament. Herod the Great was an Idumean and was therefore connected with Edom, and he sought to destroy Jesus at birth, the child who embodied all that Israel was meant to be.

Paul, too, recalls this ancient saga. He defends God's own sovereign right of election. Rebekah's two children had one and the same father, and the sons were twins. But God had determined that "the older will serve the younger" (Gen. 25:23; Rom. 9:12), in the same way that God through the prophet Malachi had said, "I have loved Jacob, but Esau I have hated" (Mal. 1:2–3).

Recommended Resource

Niehaus, J. "Obadiah." Pages 495–541 in *The Minor Prophets: An Exegetical and Expository Commentary*. Edited by T. E. McComiskey. Grand Rapids: Baker, 2009.

Questions for Review and Discussion

1. Why does Obadiah focus on the country of Edom?
2. On what grounds are we able to date the book of Obadiah?

chapter twenty-nine

THE BOOK
OF JONAH

Content: What Is Jonah About?

The book of Jonah may be divided into two major acts with two scenes each. The acts may be divided by the repetition of God's commission to the prophet in 1:1–2 and 3:1–2. The first act takes place at sea.

The first scene of the first act takes place *on* the sea, that is, on board a ship (1:1–16). The book opens with God's command to "go to the great city of Nineveh," which was geographically to the east of Israel. Rather than obeying, the narrative states that Jonah "ran away from the LORD" and boarded a ship that would take him to Tarshish, the farthest place west imaginable.

The sea has deep symbolic resonance in Scripture as a symbol of chaos, and perhaps here we are to think that Jonah thought his flight on the sea would take him beyond the control of God. If that was Jonah's thinking, he was quite wrong, because God "sent a great wind" that created "such a violent storm" that the ship was in danger. The pagan sailors react with fear, calling on their gods and working hard to keep the ship from going down, while in the meanwhile Jonah slept in the bowels of the boat. After waking him, the sailors cast lots to discover who might be to blame, and sure enough, the lots fall on Jonah. Jonah himself offers the solution: throw him overboard. The pagan sailors, however, show themselves more humane than Jonah, because they do their best to row to shore—to no avail. Then they pray to God, showing themselves to be more spiritually sensitive than Jonah, before they throw him overboard.

The second scene of the first act is *in* the sea, and more precisely, in the belly of a big fish (1:17 – 2:10). As the sea represents chaos, so its monsters, but God controls this big fish that swallows Jonah. In the fish, Jonah responds with a prayer — surprisingly, a psalm of thanksgiving — but considering the alternative, perhaps not too much so. Finally, the fish vomits Jonah onshore in the direction of Nineveh. Jonah gets the message and reluctantly sets out for that city.

In the first scene of the second act (3:1 – 10), Jonah preaches and Nineveh repents. After being vomited toward Nineveh, Jonah obeyed God by going there, but his subsequent actions make it clear that he did so only reluctantly. His message is simply, "Forty more days and Nineveh will be overthrown" (3:4), with no hint of the possibility of avoiding this fate by repentance. Like the pagan sailors, the Ninevites show themselves to be spiritually sensitive, and they repent anyway. Without guidance, though, they do not know exactly what they are doing, so they even put mourning garments on their animals. Yet God understands their hearts, and he relents from his judgment (3:10).

The second scene of the second act (4:1 – 11) finds Jonah angry and depressed over God's compassion toward the Ninevites. His reasons may be multiple, and they are unstated. Perhaps he did not want the oppressive Ninevites to have a second chance; perhaps he worried about being thought of as a false prophet whose prediction of Nineveh's fall did not materialize. In any case, this scene — and indeed the entire book — places Jonah, and perhaps God's people in general, in a bad light as not happy about God's compassion toward repentant Gentiles. God gives Jonah an object lesson by causing a plant to grow up and shield him from the sun. Jonah enjoys that plant, but then God destroys it, sending Jonah again into a bad mood. God creates an analogy between the plant and the Ninevites, saying that it is more appropriate that he love them, since they are his creation too. God's compassion toward them makes sense.

Authorship and Date: Who Wrote Jonah and When?

Jonah contains no indication of the author or the date of its composition. Jonah himself was a real prophet who lived during the reign of Jeroboam II (786 – 746 BC). He was from Gath-Hepher (el-Meshded), northeast of Nazareth. According to 2 Kings 14:25, he prophesied the expansion of the northern kingdom, which took place during Jeroboam's reign.

Genre: What Style of Literature Is Jonah?

The book of Jonah is unique among the Minor Prophets for being a narration about a prophet rather than a collection of prophetic oracles. The prose of the book is highly literary and tightly composed. This concern for rhetoric may be seen in the strategic repetition of certain key terms that provide a thread through the book or a single episode of the book. For instance, one of these key terms is the verb "rise up" (*qum*). In 1:2 God commands Jonah, "Arise, go to Nineveh" (KJV; many other translations simply say, "Go"). The next verse begins in a way that would lead the reader to expect a typical command-fulfillment pattern — "Jonah rose up ..." (KJV), but instead of completing this sentence with the expected "to go to Nineveh," the author-narrator inserts "and headed for Tarshish." We still have God's initial command to Jonah to "rise up" ringing in our minds when we hear the captain of the ship tell Jonah, "Arise, call upon thy god" (1:6 KJV). Later on, in 3:2–3, when Jonah is in the belly of the "great fish," God commissions the prophet a second time by repeating his command, "Arise, go unto Nineveh" (KJV). This time Jonah obeys: he "arose and went."

The most controversial question regarding the genre of Jonah is whether this narrative is historical or parabolic. The mention of the prophet in the historical books (2 Kings 14:25) supports the former identification, as does the fact that the prose is similar to other historical narration in the Bible. Some would argue that Jesus was treating Jonah as a historical report in Matthew 12:39–40 and Luke 11:29–30.

Others believe that the book is not a simple historical report but more like a parable or a fictional narrative that is interested in a theological message that is not dependent on its actually having happened. Of course, some simply find the story of a man being swallowed by a big fish and surviving implausible, but for those who believe God can do anything, this is not an obstacle. Still, even among those who have no problem believing that Jonah could have survived in the belly of a fish, there are some who argue that the genre signals point to a nonhistorical narrative of some sort. For instance, the reference to a "king of Nineveh" is unusual; the more typical reference would be to a "king of Assyria." Also, this king is not given a name, rendering the story (intentionally?) vague. Second, the highly literary nature of the book may also indicate that it is not historical at least in its details (see also Job).

In the final analysis, it is impossible to be dogmatic on this issue. Fortunately, the question of the intention of historicity is totally without effect on the interpretation of the book's theological message or even the exegesis of individual passages. While the historicity of much of the Old Testament is crucial to its theological significance (for instance, the Exodus), Jonah is not such a book. It is best to allow for a variety of views on the subject.

Connections: How Does Jonah Anticipate the Gospel?

Jonah anticipates the gospel in its depiction of God's concern for Gentiles, as noted above in regard to the pagan sailors and the king and inhabitants of Nineveh. As Jonah himself declared—though unhappily—God indeed is "gracious and compassionate" (4:2). While this concern for the Gentiles is rooted in the ancient covenant with Abraham (Gen. 12:3) and found elsewhere in the Old Testament, it is not a frequent theme. The New Testament, of course, is that time when Jesus breaks down "the dividing wall of hostility" between Jew and Gentile (Eph. 2:14).

Jesus compared and contrasted himself in Matthew 12:38–45 (see also Luke 11:24–32) with Jonah. When asked for a miraculous sign, he said that he would be three days and three nights in the earth (in reference to the time period between his crucifixion and resurrection [Luke 24:46]), comparable to Jonah's three days in the belly of the fish. While some believe that this analogy demands that Jonah's story is historical, Jesus' point is just as true and understandable if it is rather a parable-like story. But Jesus is not just making a simple equation between himself and Jonah. Indeed, he is "greater than Jonah" (Matt. 12:41), since, while Jonah preached to the Ninevites against his will, Jesus voluntarily gave up his life to save many.

Recommended Resources

Baldwin, J. "Jonah." Pages 543–90 in *The Minor Prophets: An Exegetical and Expository Commentary*. Edited by T. E. McComiskey. Grand Rapids: Baker, 2009.

Estelle, B. D. *Salvation through Judgment and Mercy: The Gospel according to Jonah*. Phillipsburg, NJ: P and R Publishing, 2005.

Walton, J. H. "Jonah." Pages 100–119 in ZIBBC 5. Edited by J. H. Walton. Grand Rapids: Zondervan, 2009.

Questions for Reflection and Discussion

1. Evaluate the arguments in favor of and against the identification of the book as history. In what ways, if any, does the historicity of the book affect the message of the book?
2. Assess the book of Jonah as a literary composition. What can you say about its genre, structure, and style?
3. Compare and contrast Jonah with the Gentile characters in the story.
4. How does the Jonah story fit into its time period as indicated by the reference to Jonah in 2 Kings 14:25?
5. In your opinion, does the analogy that Jesus makes between himself and Jonah (Matt. 12:38–45; Luke 11:24–32) require that the story of Jonah be historical? Why or why not?

chapter thirty

THE BOOK
OF MICAH

Content: What Is Micah About?

Micah is an eighth-century BC prophet who speaks words of judgment against both the northern and southern kingdoms, but also comes with a message of hope beyond the judgment for God's people. The structure of the book of Micah is not immediately obvious, and in fact the book is not ordered chronologically or strictly thematically. However, this collection of prophetic oracles generally falls into two cycles of judgment followed by salvation.

The first round encompasses the first five chapters. Chapters 1–3 are judgment oracles. The prophet, who acts like a covenant lawyer, begins by calling God to the witness stand. He is going to come in judgment because of the sins of both the North (Samaria) and the South (Jerusalem). The highlighted sin is false worship, and the result will be destruction. Chapter 1 lists cities that we know were on the line of march when Sennacherib and his Assyrian army threatened Judah and Jerusalem in 701 BC (vv. 10–16). The comments are based on various wordplays, such as when the prophet tells the people of Beth Ophrah ("house of dust") to go "roll in the dust" (v. 10).

Micah in particular goes after the religious leaders of God's people. The prophets, for instance, are just in it for the money (2:6–11; 3:5–7). The priests are no better (3:11), and the political leaders are unjust (3:1–3, 9–10). For these reasons, both the northern and southern kingdoms will be destroyed.

The judgment speeches of the first round are followed by salvation oracles (chaps. 4–5), beginning with the memorable picture of the temple mound being elevated to become the highest point on earth, with countless people streaming there to worship God. The result will be peace and prosperity (4:1–5). God will grant peace to his people, particularly in the face of Assyria (5:5b–15).

God begins the second round of judgment and salvation oracles by initiating a legal dispute against Israel (6:1–8). In what are perhaps the best-known verses of the book, God announces that he does not care about sacrificial offerings, but rather virtues like justice, mercy, and humility (vv. 6–8). However, Israel practices injustice, fraud, and deceit (vv. 9–16). The prophet, accordingly, laments the sins of God's people (7:1–7). Even so, the book ends with great hope as it pictures the salvation that will come to God's people after they experience the judgment coming on them due to their sin (7:8–20).

Authorship and Date: Who Wrote Micah and When?

As with most prophetic books, Micah begins with a superscription that names the prophet as well as the kings during whose reigns he ministered. The prophet is Micah of Moresheth. Micah is a common name in the Old Testament, meaning "Who is like Yahweh?" Moresheth is a city about twenty-five miles southwest of Jerusalem, located near the hills of the Shephelah. The prophet Micah is only mentioned elsewhere in Jeremiah 26:17–19. When the officials and the people wanted to put Jeremiah to death for his oracles of judgment, some unnamed elders stepped forward and defended him by citing the precedent of Micah who, they said, prophesied God's judgment against Hezekiah's Judah (they cite 3:12). Rather than putting Jeremiah to death, Hezekiah repented and saved his kingdom. Due to the elders' brave action and speech, Jeremiah survived the death threat.

The superscription lists Jotham (750–732 BC), Ahaz (732–716 BC), and Hezekiah (715–686 BC) as the kings who ruled Judah during Micah's period of ministry. Of course, he likely began toward the end of Jotham's reign and ended at the beginning of Hezekiah's reign, making him a contemporary of Isaiah. The reference to the coming judgment of Samaria (1:6) indicates that Micah's preaching began well before 722 BC, the year in which Samaria fell to the forces of Assyria. Another oracle that may be fairly well dated is the lament in 1:8–16. The cities mentioned in this section coincide with the probable route of Sennacherib's army as he approached Jerusalem in 701. And we have just observed that Jeremiah 26:18 cites Micah 3:12 as an oracle delivered during the reign of Hezekiah.

Genre: What Style of Literature Is Micah?

Micah's superscription names the contents of the book "the word of the LORD," a way of referring to a collection of prophetic oracles. The book is written exclusively in poetry. Micah offers both judgment and salvation oracles.

Connections: How Does Micah Anticipate the Gospel?

Micah addressed his oracles to Israel and Judah in their immediate historical context. But the New Testament authors recognized that his words resonated beyond his near future and applied to the great events that unfolded in their time period. The gospel of Matthew cites Micah 5:2 in reference to Jesus' birth in Bethlehem (see Matt. 2:5–6). In its Micah context, the oracle looks forward to a future David-like ruler. That is the significance of the Bethlehem birthplace.

Micah 4:1–5 evokes the picture of the exalted mountain of God and a time when the peoples of the world will flock to the worship of God. There will be peace and no war. This oracle is introduced by the rubric "in the last days." As redemptive history unfolds, it appears that this prophecy finds several anticipatory fulfillments before its ultimate fulfillment in the final days.

Recommended Resources

Longman, T. "Micah." Pages 659–764 in *Evangelical Old Testament Commentary*. Edited by W. A. Elwell. Grand Rapids: Baker, 1989.

Waltke, B. W. "Micah." Pages 591–764 in *The Minor Prophets: An Exegetical and Expository Commentary*. Edited by T. E. McComiskey. Grand Rapids: Baker, 2009.

Questions for Review and Discussion

1. What can be said about the structure of the book of Micah?
2. What is the primary charge that Micah brings against God's people?
3. During what time period did Micah prophesy? What was happening in Israel and the Near East at the time?
4. How does Micah anticipate the gospel?

chapter thirty-one

THE BOOK OF NAHUM

Content: What Is Nahum About?

The book of Nahum delivers a hard-hitting oracle announcing the demise of the city of Nineveh, the capital city of Assyria. Assyria was a superpower that oppressed many other nations including Judah, so the announcement of its end would have been received with great joy.

After the superscription (1:1), the book presents a powerful hymn extolling God the Divine Warrior (1:2–8). When God appears, mountains melt and rivers dry up. This picture of God leads naturally to a series of interwoven judgment and salvation oracles meant for Nineveh and Judah respectively, though the precise identification of the object of God's actions is not clear until the end of this section (1:9–2:2). Nahum then describes the future fall of Nineveh as if it is happening before his eyes (2:3–10; an event vision), followed by a taunt that ridicules the "lion" Nineveh (2:11–13).

Chapter 3 begins with a woe oracle, the type of speech that is spoken at a funeral. The implied funeral is for Nineveh, a city as good as dead (vv. 1–3). After this comes a second taunt against Nineveh, which is called a sorceress and harlot, and the city will suffer the punishment of a harlot for her crimes (3:4–7). More taunts follow, including one that ridicules its presumption that it is invulnerable by reminding it of the Assyrian defeat of the Egyptian city of Thebes that thought itself invulnerable (3:8–10). The rest of the chapter is filled with various insults directed toward Nineveh (3:11–17), but Nahum concludes with a dirge that rejoices at Nineveh's end (3:18–19). After all, who has not heard of their continual cruelty?

Authorship and Date: Who Wrote Nahum and When?

The superscription (1:1) names Nahum of Elkosh as the author of this book. Unfortunately, Nahum is not mentioned elsewhere, and Elkosh could be one of a number of places known by that name, though it is most likely in Judah.

The date of the book can be determined, at least in broad outline, by historical references. In the first place, Nahum announces the end of Nineveh, which we know happened at the hands of the Babylonians and Medes in 612 BC. Assuming that Nahum is true prophecy, this means that the book had to be written before that date. The mention of the fall of Thebes (3:8–10) indicates it had to be written after that event (664 BC). Thus, the date of the book is between 664 and 612 BC. Perhaps we can date it before 630, since 1:12 refers to Nineveh as intact and secure. After 630 BC, Assyria began to decline.

Genre: What Style of Literature Is Nahum?

The superscription (1:1) refers to the contents as a "book," "vision," and "oracle." Nahum is a "book," pointing to the fact that it is a literary prophecy. Most biblical prophets spoke their prophetic word and then wrote it down. Nahum's prophecy was written down from the start, as we can tell from a number of literary devices that only work in written form and not in oral speech. The terms "vision" and "oracle" address the prophetic nature of the book. An oracle is a divine utterance that concerns the future. In particular, this word occurs in contexts where a prophet speaks against a foreign nation (Isa. 13:1; 15:1; 17:1; 19:1; 21:1, 11, 13; 22:1; 23:1; 30:6; Hab. 1:1; Zech. 9:1; 12:1; Mal. 1:1); thus it might be best to translate or at least understand this term and the book of Nahum as a "war oracle" against Nineveh.

Connections: How Does Nahum Anticipate the Gospel?

Many find the book of Nahum irrelevant and a few even repulsive as it rejoices in the destruction of a city like Nineveh. Those who find it repulsive did not suffer at the hands of these violent oppressors as had Israel and Judah. Others think it is irrelevant because it speaks of God's action in the far distant past. While that is true, his actions here are illustrative of his divine nature that remains extremely relevant today.

The book begins with a hymn celebrating the Divine Warrior and then speaks of the warrior's actions against Nineveh. God is still a warrior today, though his battle is not against flesh and blood, but against the spiritual powers and authorities. In Paul's writings, Christ's death, resurrection, and ascension are seen as the culmination of his warfare against Satan and his cohorts (Col. 2:14–15; Eph. 4:7–10). In addition, the Old Testament's (and Nahum's) picture of God as warrior and Christ's warfare against Satan anticipate the consummation of this theme in the book of Revelation (see, for instance, Rev. 19:11–21), when evil comes to an end as Jesus leads his army in the final battle against Satan and his demonic and human army. Thus, although Nineveh no longer exists, the abiding significance of the book of Nahum is found in the warring Christ of the New Testament.

Recommended Resources

Longman, T. "Nahum." Pages 765–829 in *The Minor Prophets: An Exegetical and Expository Commentary*. Edited by T. E. McComiskey. Grand Rapids: Baker, 2009.

Longman, T., and D. Reid. *God Is a Warrior*. Grand Rapids: Zondervan, 1995.

Questions for Review and Discussion

1. How would you summarize Nahum's prophetic message?
2. What is the significance of Nineveh in Nahum's prophecy?
3. What message does Nahum have for Judah?
4. How can Nahum's violent prophecy anticipate the gospel?

chapter thirty-two

THE BOOK
OF HABAKKUK

Content: What Is Habakkuk About?

The book begins with a typical prophetic superscription naming Habakkuk as the source of the oracles that follow, and then the prophet engages in an interchange with God. Habakkuk twice complains about God's ways. In the first complaint, the prophet asks God why he tolerates injustice where the wicked frustrate God's law so that they can perpetuate violence against the righteous (1:2–4). The reference to "law" reveals that this complaint arises from injustices within Judean society. God's response is surprising and unsettling. He announces that he is raising up the Babylonians to execute his judgment against the sinners (1:5–2:5).

God's response does not satisfy Habakkuk. How can God use the evil Babylonians to respond to the sins in Judah (1:12–17)? God is going to bring judgment on the wicked, but he will do it with an instrument even more wicked than the evil in Judah. Thus those who are even more wicked will then prosper the more. God responds by saying that he will judge the unrighteous (2:1–5). The pride of Babylon will not escape his judgment (2:4–5). Human opinion about righteousness and wrong lacks the capacity to evaluate God's actions in history; those who are truly righteous must live in faithful confidence that God will keep his promises (2:4b). Just as Abraham had believed God and had been credited with righteousness (Gen. 15:6), the prophet too must continue to have confidence in God.

The prophet then launches into a series of woe oracles (2:6–20), the form for which derives from funeral rituals and which thus state

171

that the object of the oracle is as good as dead. The wicked will not always prosper. No, the plunderer will be plundered (2:6–8), the conqueror will be shamed (2:9–11), the builder will be undone (2:12–14), the shameless will be shamed (2:15–18), and the idolater will be silenced (2:19–20).

The third and final chapter presents a hymn, a victory song describing the appearance of the Divine Warrior in his war chariot. This song is written in a form that resembles ancient Hebrew style and is either consciously archaized by the prophet or was written earlier and included by him as appropriate for his message. At God's coming, the heavens and the earth convulse (3:3–7). The Lord shows his dominion over the chaotic waters as he had done at creation; he comes with his weapons to judge the nations as he had done at the exodus (3:8–15). Habakkuk takes confidence from the deeds in the past and will "wait patiently for the day of calamity to come on the nation invading us" (3:16).

Authorship and Date: Who Wrote Habakkuk and When?

The superscription (1:1) names Habakkuk as the author of the oracles and hymn in the book. While no specific historical context is added, the fact that God was "raising up the Babylonians" (1:6) at this time indicates that Habakkuk prophesied sometime after 626, when — according to ancient Near Eastern sources — Nabopolassar proclaimed himself king of Babylon and began his revolt against Assyrian hegemony. That Habakkuk looks to God's use of Babylon as a future agent of judgment against Judah suggests that the prophecy was given before the destruction of Jerusalem in 586 BC. Such a dating makes Habakkuk a contemporary of Jeremiah, Ezekiel, Nahum, and Zephaniah.

Genre: What Style of Literature Is Habakkuk?

Habakkuk is a prophetic book that uses a dialogue form at the beginning, where the prophet's laments elicit a response from Yahweh that reveals his future judging activity. The prophet also utilizes the "woe oracle," which derives from funeral ritual and was a common prophetic way of announcing that the object of God's wrath is as good as dead. The book ends with a hymn celebrating the future victory of the Divine Warrior over the forces of evil.

Connections: How Does Habakkuk Anticipate the Gospel?

The apostle Paul admonishes Christians that Jesus has called his followers to a life of faith. He appeals to Habakkuk (2:4) in his argument that righteousness—from first to last, for Abraham, Job, Habakkuk, and for all—is by faith (Rom. 1:17). Although we live in a present evil age (Gal. 1:4), "the righteous will live by faith" (Gal. 3:11). Faith is "confidence in what we hope for and assurance about what we do not see" (Heb. 11:1). The ancients were commended for believing God when the circumstances all conspired to say that such faith would not be rewarded (Heb. 11:2–40). We too are called to that same faith, for God will yet come as the Divine Warrior and will vindicate his name (Rev. 19:11–16).

Recommended Resources

Bruce, F. F. "Habakkuk." Pages 831–96 in *The Minor Prophets: An Exegetical and Expository Commentary*. Edited by T. E. McComiskey. Grand Rapids: Baker, 2009.

Bruckner, J. *Jonah, Nahum, Habakkuk, Zephaniah*. NIVAC. Grand Rapids: Zondervan, 2004.

Questions for Review and Discussion

1. Habakkuk preaches against injustice. Where does he see injustice, and how does he ask God to respond to it?
2. During what time period did Habakkuk prophesy? How do we know?
3. What literary forms does Habakkuk use to communicate his message?
4. Why does Habakkuk include a hymn celebrating the Divine Warrior at the end of his prophecy?
5. How does Paul use Habakkuk to insist that righteousness is by faith? What does he mean by this?

chapter thirty-three

THE BOOK
OF ZEPHANIAH

Content: What Is Zephaniah About?

Zephaniah shares many of the concerns of his contemporary prophetic colleagues. Judah has sinned and deserves God's judgment. The book begins with a statement announcing universal judgment. God will sweep the world clean of its pervasive wickedness (1:2–3). After giving this broad perspective, Zephaniah then narrows in on Judah. God will purge Judah and Jerusalem of those who worship foreign gods, such as Baal and Molek. He will offer them up like a sacrifice (1:4–9). The day of judgment is coming for Jerusalem in which the wealthy are singled out in particular (1:10–13). Zephaniah uses the common prophetic concept of the Day of the Lord to describe the coming debacle (first found at Amos 5:18–24). This day is the point when God himself will come to judge the wicked, though perhaps those who "seek righteousness" (2:3) will be spared (1:14–2:3).

As with many other prophets, Zephaniah's message extends beyond the confines of Judah to take in all the other nations. He thus delivers oracles against Philistia (2:4–7), Moab and Ammon (2:8–11), Cush (2:12), and Assyria (2:13–15) before returning again to Jerusalem (3:1–7), and he summarizes this section with a statement again (as in 1:2–3) announcing universal judgment (3:8).

Typical of many prophets, Zephaniah looks beyond the horizon of judgment to see future restoration. As there was universal judgment, so in the future there will be universal worship (3:9–10). The book ends with oracles anticipating restoration of and blessing upon Judah (3:11–20).

Authorship and Date: Who Wrote Zephaniah and When?

The superscription names Zephaniah as the author of the oracles contained in this book. He is given an extensive genealogy that connects him four generations back to Hezekiah, almost certainly the king who reigned over Judah from 727 to 698 BC. Thus Zephaniah was a member of the extended royal family. The superscription also specifies that he ministered during the reign of King Josiah of Judah (640–609 BC), the only question being during what part of his reign, before or after this pious king's efforts to bring back the proper worship of the Lord. There is no mention of the discovery of the law book that happened in 621 BC. In addition, Zephaniah rebukes those who worship false gods. These facts lead some to believe that Zephaniah ministered before the reforms got seriously under way. On the other hand, the fact that those who worshiped Baal are referred to as a "remnant" may indicate that Josiah had already begun his purge of false religion in his reign. In the final analysis, we cannot be sure when within the reign of Josiah Zephaniah prophesied. He was a contemporary or near contemporary of Jeremiah, Ezekiel, Nahum, and Habakkuk.

Genre: What Style of Literature Is Zephaniah?

Zephaniah is a prophetic book. It contains oracles against the nations (see Obadiah) as well as both judgment speeches and salvation oracles that announced future punishment and restoration respectively.

Connections: How Does Zephaniah Anticipate the Gospel?

Christian readers recognize in Zephaniah many images and motifs that are also used in the New Testament. Zephaniah anticipated an imminent historical threat and outbreak of divine judgment. This historical outbreak of the day of the Lord in the Babylonian conquest and exile was but a foretaste of that great and terrible day on an eschatological and cosmic scale. Paul writes often of the Day of the Lord, the day of Christ (Rom. 2:16; 1 Cor. 1:8; Phil. 1:6, 10; 2:16; 2 Tim. 4:8), and looks for that final theophany and vindication of God in history. John describes the Warrior God coming with his armies to execute judgment (Rev. 19:11–16). Zephaniah had announced a terrible sacrifice that God himself would offer (1:7), and John makes use of the same image when he describes the Day of the Lord (Rev. 19:17–18; cf. Ezek. 39:18–20).

Along with other prophets, Zephaniah looked to a day when all nations would acknowledge and worship the God of Israel (3:9–10). For the church, the new Israel composed of Jew and Gentile alike (Gal. 3:8–9, 14, 26–29), this is present reality. The church, too, lives with the knowledge and hope that the world will yet acknowledge the rule of its true King (Phil. 2:9–11).

Recommended Resource

Baker, D. W. *Nahum, Habakkuk, and Zephaniah*. TOTC. Downers Grove, IL: InterVarsity Press, 1988.

Questions for Reflection and Discussion

1. According to Zephaniah, against whom will God bring judgment and why?
2. During what time period did Zephaniah prophesy? What was going on at the time?
3. What is the Day of the Lord in Zephaniah and how does this day anticipate the New Testament?

chapter thirty-four

THE BOOK
OF HAGGAI

Content: What Is Haggai About?

After the book's superscription (1:1), in the first oracle (1:2–11) Haggai challenges the viewpoint that the time was not right to build the temple. Haggai dates this oracle to the first day of the sixth month of the second year of the Persian king Darius (August 29, 520 BC). He points out that they seem to be able to find the resources and the time to build their own houses, and he implies that God's house comes first. He also reminds them that their lack of crops, drink, clothes, and wages is not an excuse to avoid finishing the building, but rather a consequence of their not getting on with the task.

While most prophets had their messages rejected, 1:12–15 records that Zerubbabel, the central leader of the early postexilic period, and the people got the message. They began work again on the temple on the twenty-fourth day of the sixth month of Darius's second year (twenty-three days later; September 21, 520 BC).

A month after work resumed on the temple (the twenty-first day of the seventh month of the same year; October 17, 520 BC), Haggai delivered a second oracle (2:1–9). This day would have been the last of the Festival of Tabernacles (Lev. 23:33–43; Num. 29:12–39; Deut. 16:13–15; Ezek. 45:23–25). Now that the building had begun again, it was clear to those who knew the first temple that this second temple would not be as grand, and Haggai encourages them in their disappointment. He tells them that the glory of this temple will actually exceed that of the first temple (2:6–9).

Haggai's third and fourth oracles (2:10–19, 20–23) are both delivered on the same day (the twenty-fourth day of the ninth month of the same year; December 18, 520 BC), three months after the work on the temple had begun. The third oracle has two parts: (1) a question about Torah (2:10–14) cast in the form of the dialogue between Yahweh and the prophet, and (2) a message of encouragement (2:15–19). The point of the ruling on the legal question is that holiness is not contagious—just working on the temple would not make the people holy—but ritual uncleanness or defilement is contagious, and the temple itself could be defiled by the uncleanness of the people. The only hope the nation had for divine approval and acceptance was the grace of God. The temple would not be a magical talisman. Perhaps, in the three months since the work began, the people had become a bit discouraged, and the prophet encourages them in their work with assurances of divine blessing. December was the middle of the growing season, and the prophet assures the people that time away from farmwork to work on the temple would not mean a poor harvest, but to the contrary, a great harvest lay ahead (cf. 1:5–11).

Haggai's fourth oracle (2:20–23) is addressed to Zerubbabel, the governor of Judah and a descendant in the line of David through Jehoiachin. In the book of Jeremiah, God had earlier described Jehoiachin as a signet ring on his hand (Jer. 22:24–25), a ring that would be pulled off and discarded. In Haggai, God uses the same imagery, but reverses it, this time describing a descendant of Jehoiachin as a valued signet ring on the hand of God. Although Haggai, Zechariah, and their contemporaries may have hoped for the overthrow of foreign domination and the restoration of Davidic rule in their own day, Zerubbabel would not be this Davidic king; instead, they pointed forward to an eschatological day when God would shake the heavens and the earth (2:6–7, 21).

Authorship and Date: Who Wrote Haggai and When?

The book named after Haggai identifies him as the author of its oracles. Since the framework refers to Haggai in the third person, many scholars have concluded that he was not himself the author of the book, but that an editor set the prophet's utterances into their narrative context. Of course, Haggai could have authored the narrative himself, choosing the third-person narratives in the framework in order to enhance the objectivity and historical reality of the report or to authenticate his oracles as the word of God.

Haggai, like Ezekiel, gives precise dates for his oracles (see above), all in the second year of Darius (520 BC). After the Persians defeated the Babylonians and Cyrus issued a decree allowing the Jewish people to return to Judah, the people had come back with the mandate to build the temple. However, they paused in their efforts, and God sent Haggai along with Zechariah to encourage them to finish the work (see Ezra 5:1). The people responded well and began immediately and finished the work in 515 BC.

Genre: What Style of Literature Is Haggai?

Haggai is a prophetic book composed of four oracles (1:1 – 11; 2:1 – 9, 10 – 19, 20 – 23), with the first and the second divided by a short narrative describing the reaction to the first oracle (1:12 – 15).

Connections: How Does Haggai Anticipate the Gospel?

Haggai's prophetic burden focuses on the temple. The Babylonians had destroyed the first temple in 586 BC. The prophet understands the importance of the temple for the relationship between God and his people. After all, it reflects his presence among them. To meet with God, the Jewish people had to go to the temple.

In the New Testament we see that Jesus likewise respected the temple as his Father's house (John 2:12 – 25). However, he also spoke of its future destruction (Mark 13:2), and he is reported to have said, "I will destroy this temple made with human hands and in three days will build another, not made with hands" (Mark 14:58). After Jesus' death (accompanied by the splitting of the curtain of the temple; Matt. 27:51), it became clear to his disciples that Jesus himself was the presence of God fulfilling the promise of the temple, so that the temple was no longer needed. Jesus was the very presence of God, who "tabernacled in our midst, and we beheld his glory" (John 1:14, author's translation), for he was "the radiance of God's glory and the exact representation of his being" (Heb. 1:3). This is but a step toward the consummation, when all things will be new and the dwelling of God will be with people in a city rich beyond description, where all tears are wiped away (Rev. 21).

Recommended Resources

Boda, M. J. *Haggai, Zechariah*. NIVAC. Grand Rapids: Zondervan, 2004.

Motyer, J. A. "Haggai." Pages 963–1002 in *The Minor Prophets: An Exegetical and Expository Commentary.* Edited by T. E. McComiskey. Grand Rapids: Baker, 2009.

Questions for Reflection and Discussion

1. During what time period did Haggai prophesy? What was going on at the time?
2. What is Haggai's main message?
3. What role does Zerubbabel play in Haggai's message?
4. What is the relationship between Jesus and the temple?

chapter thirty-five

THE BOOK
OF ZECHARIAH

Content: What Is Zechariah About?

The book of Zechariah may be divided into two parts. Chapters 1–8 concern matters in the prophet's immediate historical horizon, while chapters 9–14 look into the far distant future through the use of eschatological imagery.

The first part itself begins, after the superscription (1:1; see below), with the prophet asserting his authority as being in line with the prophets who preceded him (1:2–6). This oracle is dated to the eighth month of the second year of Darius (October/November 520 BC). Zechariah speaks on behalf of the Lord Almighty, and he warns the people not to ignore his prophetic word the way that their forefathers ignored the clear call of the earlier prophets. After this admonition, Zechariah describes his eight night visions (1:7–6:8).

The first night vision (1:7–17) is dated to the twenty-fourth day of the eleventh month of the second year of Darius (Feb. 15, 519 BC). In this vision Zechariah sees a man riding a red horse, standing behind myrtle trees in a ravine. Behind him are red, brown, and white horses. These are God's agents who survey the world on his behalf, and they now report that the nations are at ease. In answer to the prophet's question, the angel of the Lord—perhaps to be identified with the rider on the red horse—intercedes with God to show mercy to his people, especially considering the fact that the nations around them are experiencing peace and quiet. God responds by saying he will restore prosperity to his people and at the same time bring judgment on the nations. The second night vision (1:18–21) concerns four horns, symbols of power, that have scattered God's people—an obvious reference to nations like Babylon that God used as a tool of his judgment. The vision then describes four craftsmen who will destroy the horns. While the details of the symbolism are obscure, the message is clear: God will destroy those nations that have harassed his people.

The third night vision (2:1–13) describes a man with a measuring line, who will take the dimensions of Jerusalem, presumably in anticipation of rebuilding. The angel of the Lord informs him that the lack of walls, rather than being a weakness, is a sign of its prosperity. Rather than a physical wall, God will protect Jerusalem with a ball of fire, an expression of his glorious presence. The imagery is that of the entire city being taken within the pillars of fire, the Shekinah glory; no longer is the presence of God confined to the Most Holy Place within the temple, but instead, the entire city has become the dwelling place of God. The fourth night vision (3:1–10) pictures the high priest, Joshua, standing before God in filthy clothes. An accuser—"Satan" means "accuser"—charges him with sin, represented by his filthy garments. But rather than convicting Joshua, God rebukes Satan for accusing a "burning stick snatched from the fire" (3:2). God then puts clean clothes on the priest, representing a righteousness not his own, and admonishes him to be obedient. In the context of the historical events of Zechariah's own day, the high priest represents the nation; his cleansing by God affirms that the returnees of that generation will be able to build an acceptable temple for God.

In the fifth night vision (4:1–14) the prophet sees a lampstand consisting of a single basin with seven lamps around its rim, each having spouts for seven wicks, so that there would be a total of forty-nine flames. The oil for the lamp comes from olive trees and clusters of fruit in the background. Pipes deliver the oil from the trees directly to the lamp. The priests used to tend the lampstands in the temple twice a day, once in the morning and again in the evening, trimming the wicks and refilling the lamps with oil. Here was a lampstand that did not need human tending. The point of the vision is clear: the work on the temple is God's work (4:6) that he will see to completion (4:9). Zerubbabel, the governor, and Joshua, the priest, are the "two olive branches beside the two gold pipes that pour out golden oil" (4:12); they will be the ones to complete the task of rebuilding the temple.

The sixth and seventh night visions are related in that both symbolically refer to sin remaining within the restoration community that needs to be eradicated. The sixth (5:1–4) is a flying scroll on which are written curses against a thief and a blasphemer, summarizing the Ten Commandments as offenses against humans (commandments 5–10) and God (commandments 1–4). The seventh vision (5:5–11) symbolizes evil in the community as a woman in a basket, which will be sent back to Babylon where it belongs.

The eighth and final vision (6:1–8) returns to the theme of horses that roam the earth. The details are unclear, but the central point is obvious: God will avenge himself by punishing the nations.

The rest of the first part of the book concerns reports or historical events. In 6:9–15, some exiles visit Jerusalem and bring gifts of silver and gold for the temple from some Jews who still live in exile. They take these metals and put a crown on Joshua, the high priest, who here is called the Branch (previously used for Joshua in 3:8). Although the title "Branch" and the reference to crowns are meant for rulers (like Zerubbabel), here we have the blending of the offices of the priest and the king, which Christian interpreters have taken as an anticipation of the Messiah.

In 7:1–3 we hear of a delegation that arrives at the temple on the fourth day of the ninth month of the fourth year of Darius (Dec. 7, 518 BC). They ask the priests—now that the exile is completed and the temple is almost rebuilt—whether they should continue to fast as they had through the exile on dates that commemorated events surrounding the destruction of Jerusalem. Zechariah uses the occasion to critique their hypocritical observance of religion and to encourage them to show obedience from the heart (7:4–8:23). He ends with the anticipation of the day when Gentiles will worship along with Israel (8:20–23; see also 14:16–21).

In the second part of the book (chaps. 9–14), the prophet's vision extends to the far distant future. Notwithstanding all that the return from the exile represents, a yet fuller redemption still lies ahead. While some argue that the focus, literary forms, and language of these two parts of Zechariah are so different, others point to deep thematic connections between the two in order to argue for their authorial unity. These include (1) the importance assigned to Jerusalem (1:12–16; 2:1–13; 9:8–10; 12:1–13; 14:1–21); (2) the cleansing of the community (3:1–9; 5:1–11; 10:9; 12:10; 13:1–2; 14:20–21); (3) the place of the Gentiles in the kingdom of God (2:11; 8:20–23; 9:7, 10; 14:1–4); (4) dependence on the works of the former prophets (1:4; Isa. 58 in 7:4–10; Amos 1:9–10 and 5:27–6:2 in 9:1–8; Jer. 25:34–38 in 11:1–3; Ezek. 47:1–10 in 14:1–4); (5) the restoration of paradisiacal fertility (8:12; 14:8); (6) renewal of the covenant (8:8; 13:9); (7) the regathering of the exiles (2:6; 8:7; 10:9–10); (8) the outpouring of the Spirit (4:6; 12:10); and (9) the coming of the Messiah (3:8; 4:6; 9:9–10). (For more on chapters 9–14, see Connections below.)

Authorship and Date: Who Wrote Zechariah and When?

The superscription (1:1) names Zechariah as the author of the "word of the LORD" contained in the book of his name. He is identified as a son of Berekiah, the son of Iddo, and is named only in Ezra 5:1 and 6:14 and Nehemiah 12:16, where he and Haggai are named as prophets proclaiming God's will that the people complete the construction of the temple, a message in keeping with many of the oracles that are included in the book. His mention in Nehemiah 12:16 also indicates that he is a priest, which makes sense of why he answers an inquiry directed to priests in chapters 7–8.

Like Haggai, Zechariah utilizes date formulae in his book. He does so three times, dating his opening words (1:2–6) to the eighth month of Darius's second year (October/November 520 BC), his first night vision to the twenty-fourth day of the eleventh month of Darius's second year (Feb. 15, 519 BC), and the inquiry into fasting to the fourth day of the ninth month of Darius's fourth year (Dec. 7, 518 BC).

Genre: What Style of Literature Is Zechariah?

Zechariah identifies the content of his book as the "word of the LORD" (1:1), indicating prophetic oracles of judgment and salvation. After an opening admonition to heed his message (1:2–6), there are eight night visions in which the prophet sees something that is enigmatic to him, but is explained by an angelic interpreter (1:7–6:8). Zechariah 6:9–10 is a historical report about returning exiles bringing a gift for the temple (6:9–15), while the first part of the book ends with a response to an inquiry directed at the priests, which turns into an admonition to be obedient to God, not just in behavior but also in heart (7:1–8:13). Finally, there are two oracles (chaps. 9–11; chaps. 12–14) about Israel's enemies and the coming of Zion's king and shepherd.

Connections: How Does Zechariah Anticipate the Gospel?

Christian readers of Zechariah cannot but notice that the coming age of full redemption is inaugurated by a messianic king who makes a humble appearance, bringing righteousness and salvation to Jerusalem while riding on a donkey (9:9; Matt. 21:5). He is the shepherd king, but a smitten shepherd (13:7; Matt. 26:31), betrayed and pierced (11:12–13; 12:10; Matt. 26:15; 27:9–10; John 19:34, 37). Yet it is this King who will subdue the nations (12:8–9) and establish his kingdom among humankind (14:3–9).

Recommended Resources

Boda, M. J. *Haggai, Zechariah*. NIVAC. Grand Rapids: Zondervan, 2004.

Gregory, B. R. *Longing for God in an Age of Discouragement: The Gospel according to Zechariah*. Phillipsburg, NJ: P and R Publishing, 2010.

McComiskey, T. E. "Zechariah." Pages 1003–1244 in *The Minor Prophets: An Exegetical and Expository Commentary*. Edited by T. E. McComiskey. Grand Rapids: Baker, 2009.

Questions for Reflection and Discussion

1. What are the major themes of Zechariah's night visions?
2. What role does the temple play in Zechariah's message?
3. How does Zechariah 1–8 differ from 9–14?
4. When did Zechariah give his prophetic message? How does his message fit into his time period?
5. How does Jesus' life connect to the book of Zechariah?

chapter thirty-six

THE BOOK
OF MALACHI

Content: What Is Malachi About?

After the superscription, Malachi disputes the people of Israel and their leaders on six critical points. Through Malachi, God begins by challenging the people by asserting his love for them (1:2–5), to which the people express their doubt. God responds by telling them about his judgment on Edom, which has been harassing them. In the second disputation (1:6–2:9) God disputes the priests because they have shown him contempt by offering inadequate sacrifices. In the third disputation (2:10–16) God accuses his people of "profan[ing] the covenant of our ancestors" (2:10). It is unclear whether this is a specific reference to the Abrahamic covenant or the Mosaic covenant or both. God supports his accusation by the fact that Israelite men were divorcing their wives.

The fourth disputation finds God pushing back against the claim that he is unjust (2:17–3:5). God responds by saying he will come in judgment. The fifth dispute asserts that while God does not change, Israel must (3:6–12). Why do they need to change? They shortchange God in their tithes, and therefore he has withheld his blessing from them. If they change their behavior, then he will bring them surplus. Finally, in the sixth and final dispute (3:13–4:3), God accuses Israel of using harsh words against him when they say that it is futile to serve him. This statement emanates from a feeling that God is being unjust by prospering the arrogant. Again, God will make it clear in the future that he will bring prosperity to the righteous and punishment to the wicked.

A short appendix follows the disputations. Malachi 4:4 is a call to observe the law of the Lord, and 4:5–6 announces the future arrival of the prophet Elijah on the Day of the Lord. It is on this note that the book of Malachi ends, the last book of the Old Testament (according to the Greek-English tradition).

Authorship and Date: Who Wrote Malachi and When?

The superscription (1:1) states that Malachi wrote the book. Since no father or place of residence is mentioned, some scholars believe that this is not a proper name but a reference to "my messenger," the meaning of the Hebrew word, related to the messenger mentioned in 3:1. However, that figure is a future messenger and cannot be related to the person mentioned in the superscription.

Malachi and his book may be dated to the postexilic/Persian period (post–539 BC). The evidence is overwhelming. The temple has been rebuilt (accomplished in 515 BC), and the word used for "governor" (*peha*) in 1:8 is a technical term from the Persian period. However, it is not possible to be more precise, although the disillusionment concerning the temple suggests that a few decades have passed since its completion. This was a difficult time for God's people, who may have expected a more robust restoration than they experienced at this time.

Genre: What Style of Literature Is Malachi?

The superscription uses the terms "oracle" and "word of the LORD" to refer to the contents of the book, which indicate that the book contains prophetic oracles. The specific form that is characteristic of Malachi is the disputation. The first disputation (1:2–5) reveals the structure of this form. The Lord begins by asserting a truth about his nature to the people: "I have loved you." The people are then provoked to question the Lord, "How have you loved us?" The Lord responds to the challenge by describing the destruction of the Edomites, the offspring of Esau. Edom had been a particularly annoying adversary to Israel (see Obadiah), and their destruction was most welcome and to be interpreted as a sign of God's love for Israel.

Connections: How Does Malachi Anticipate the Gospel?

The gospel of Mark opens with a quotation that collages Malachi 3:1 with Isaiah 40:3:

"I will send my messenger ahead of you,
　who will prepare your way" —
"a voice of one calling in the wilderness,
'Prepare the way for the Lord,
　make straight paths for him'" (Mark 1:2–3).

In the so-called appendix to the book of Malachi, the messenger is further identified with Elijah, who will precede the Lord on the day of victory and judgment. In the New Testament the messenger who prepares the way is John the Baptist, who brings the kind of stern message of coming destruction as described in Malachi 3:1–5. He precedes and introduces Jesus' earthly ministry, and it is Jesus himself who identifies John as Elijah, whose heralding role is anticipated in Malachi (Matt. 11:7–15; see also Luke 7:18–35). In short, the eschatological hopes of the book of Malachi find their fulfillment in the pages of the Gospels.

Recommended Resource

Stuart, D. "Malachi." Pages 1245–1396 in *The Minor Prophets: An Exegetical and Expository Commentary*. Edited by T. E. McComiskey. Grand Rapids: Baker, 2009.

Questions for Reflection and Discussion

1. How does Malachi use the disputation form in support of his message?
2. What does the book of Malachi tell us about the spiritual state of the people of God?
3. When did Malachi prophesy? How does his message relate to his time period?
4. How is John the Baptist related to the message of Malachi?

SCRIPTURE INDEX

The index is not exhaustive and instead includes Scriptures that (1) are referenced in chapters devoted to a different book of the Bible, or (2) are quoted. The index also includes the pagination for entire chapters corresponding to books of the Bible.